Opening Up

Opening Up

Geoff Boycott

ARTHUR BARKER LIMITED   LONDON
A subsidiary of Weidenfeld (Publishers) Limited

Published in Great Britain by Arthur Barker Limited
91 Clapham High Street
London SW4 7TA

ISBN 0 213 16760 3

Filmset by Keyspools Ltd, Golborne, Lancs
Printed in Great Britain by
Butler & Tanner Ltd, Frome and London

Contents

1

A dirty word

A strange thing happened to the word 'professional' on its journey through modern journalism. A word which should embody everything good in sport was somehow squeezed, stretched, twisted and pummelled until it came to reflect practically everything which is seedy and pretentious in the game.

Football probably started the rot with its talk about professional fouls, professional time wasting, professional tricks of the trade which were at best gamesmanship and at worst simple, straightforward cheating. Since professional players were always excusing themselves by suggesting they were not entirely bound by the rules of the game, much less its spirit, it is not surprising that the media connected professionalism and sharp practice in the same breath. Suddenly, professionalism has become a dirty word.

Cricket cannot escape some of the stigma. A few years ago during a Test Match between South Africa and Australia an Aussie batsman nicked the ball towards slip, and there was an appeal for the catch. 'Did you catch it?' asked the batsman, unsure if it had carried. 'Sure I did,' returned the fielder and the batsman had no option but to go.

'Are you sure you caught that?' asked a dubious second slip as the batsman disappeared. 'I caught it all right ... he didn't ask me if it bounced first, did he?' came the reply. A real professional's trick, the sort of story which is accepted as part of the game today.

But that wasn't professionalism. It wasn't even gamesmanship or any other fancy word. It was just cheating. And as one who wants to be proud to call himself a professional sportsman I resent the way the word has become debased. There was a time when being a professional was a badge of honour; now it is practically an accusation.

Take a man like Rod Laver. A superb player, twice winner of the Grand Slam, universally accepted in his time as the supreme example of tennis professionalism. I never recall him as much as disputing a line call, let alone stooping to any sort of trick to win a point; he is a man who upheld the pride and dignity of his sport by the sheer depth of his ability and the near-flawlessness of his conduct.

We are not all Rod Lavers and we all make human mistakes. But all professionals have a responsibility to try, at least, try, to reflect what is best in the game. It is easy to forget what we owe.

If there is such a thing as a definition of the complete professional it is the man who does everything humanly possible to improve his game, to bring it to a peak of perfection so that he can't reproach himself by saying, 'I could have done so-and-so to make that performance better.' Perfection is the goal and the real professional is never happy with anything less than his best.

Enthusiasm communicates itself, too, and I always tell the youngsters at Yorkshire that if they are seen to be doing their best – and seen to be getting enjoyment out of it – the public will more readily forgive the days when things don't go just right. They may go away disappointed but will not be totally disheartened – and they will be back to watch again if they feel the players are really giving everything they've got. That may be a naïve point of view but our gates at Yorkshire prove it is not entirely wrong.

Perhaps it is harder for youngsters these days to discipline themselves to a really professional point of view. For a start, they have things so much easier than many great players of the past, easier than I did when I first started – and that's not the carping of an old man. We tend to think that life is more demanding, more complicated, but the fact is that it is materially easier than ever; people are better off than ever they were.

When I first started – and we are talking about 1962, not thirty or forty years ago – I used to have to catch a bus or train or cadge a lift to County matches. And that went on even after I played for England. I saved enough to buy my first car in July 1965. I wouldn't have bought one unless I could pay cash for it, and by then I had played in a dozen Test Matches.

Nowadays at Yorkshire there is hardly a second team player who does not run a car or turn up in one he's borrowed from father. No catching buses or humping heavy cases around for them. Life is that much easier. The affluent society I'm talking about has a profound effect on youngsters' ideas of professionalism because it takes a lot of fear out of the job. Yes, fear!

The old-timers who made themselves into great cricketers desperately wanted to play the game, not just for itself but because it represented a means of escape into a better way of life. Their wages could be three times as much as those earned by most working men and you can be sure they didn't want to lose out on that. There was a fear of losing their job and the life-style that went with it. Sure, it could be hard work but it was a good job compared with many others; a sight better than going down the pit. ...

Cricketers' wages have lost ground, relatively speaking, over the years. Most cricketers certainly don't earn three times the average wage today, so the game has lost its exceptional status financially and young players have lost a bit of impetus, that fear of losing a really well-paid job. If a youngster fails to make the grade his pride may suffer but he will probably find a job which is just as well paid without much difficulty.

An established county player like Robin Hobbs felt like quitting the game not so very long ago because he could earn more money in a secure, year-round job than he could playing for Essex. Admittedly, that doesn't happen very often but it does illustrate the way financial incentives have changed.

One result of this is that competition for places in County sides is less fierce than it used to be. The Yorkshire nets today aren't as competitive as they were fifteen years ago. And that means that young players need all their character if they are going to make really good professionals. It's a personal thing; a young player has to drive himself, to set his own high standards, and that is not easy.

Young people are more liberated these days. They have their cars, their girlfriends, and get out and about at an earlier age. So when they break into County cricket, staying at decent hotels and eating out quite often, they take to it like ducks to water. It easily becomes a fantasy world, a glamorously easy way of life. But it's a shabby sort of professional who can't be relied on to get himself to bed at a decent hour.

Then there is practice. I have always practised in the nets; I suppose I spend as much time in the nets as any player in the game. Not because I have an insatiable appetite for batting or because I get some sort of perverse pleasure out of making bowlers work but because there is always some specific point which can be improved, some fault which can be ironed out.

It mystifies me that so many youngsters come into the game today and say they do not like net practice. 'I've had enough of nets; nets bore me ....' they say. Well, if it bores them to have fifteen minutes in the nets, how are they ever going to bat for a full day in a Test Match? Where are they going to learn? Not in the middle, that's for sure, because that is where they have to get runs. That is no place for sorting out weaknesses.

Nets are the place to develop the right attitude to the game. Three good shots followed by one sloppy one and you are out for twelve – and that's not going to build any career. Many a good batsman has net practice simply to find or maintain his rhythm; sometimes it's a matter of concentration, but to complain that nets are boring, to become lackadaisical simply because you cannot set yourself a target and a standard – that is wholly unprofessional.

Naturally, not everybody wants or needs to spend the same amount of time in the nets; people are different and they have to assess their needs differently. But if we are talking about the real professional there is nobody, nobody, who can do without net practice altogether.

Some well known players, Barry Richards for example, tend to give the impression they are so naturally talented they don't need to practise. They do themselves a disservice and, more important perhaps, they may mislead lots of boys who admire them and want to copy their attitudes.

Gary Sobers, superb player that he was, had a reputation for being an instinctive, carefree cricketer and admitted that he didn't take easily to practice. But I remember a day in Trinidad in 1968 when I went back for extra nets and Sobers was there, out

Relaxation for them, business for me. There is always some point which can be ironed out in the nets.

of the public eye, practicing against a few local bowlers. I bowled at him myself. He knew he had to work at his job like everybody else; some don't like to admit it but every good player needs to learn, even to bring something out of himself by teaching others. Talent is important, enthusiasm is vital, practice knits them both together.

Self-discipline, practice ... and there is another professional quality which is overlooked by too many players in the game, even in the age of seven days a week cricket: fitness.

Cricket is a pretty arduous game, even if it may not always look that way. A full day in the field takes a lot out of anybody and nowadays, when limited-overs matches add to the workload and often mean a lot of travelling, fitness is more important than ever. Yet you would be surprised how many players, and young ones at that, don't take enough trouble to keep themselves fit. But attitudes are changing. Counties are becoming more aware of the importance of fitness and insisting that their players undertake regular and effective training.

If I don't go on a winter tour I spend at least a month before the season starts getting myself fit. Five days a week, in a tracksuit, doing exercises, jogging, sprints and, as always, a controlled diet. It makes a tremendous amount of difference.

Look what happened to Bob Willis of Warwickshire. Before the tour to India four years ago, Bob had had rather limited success with England. He was in and out of the side, often because he was injured. But he worked really hard to beat the knee trouble which dogged him for years, he stuck to a training programme worked out by the England physiotherapist, Bernard Thomas, and he really put himself through it. He was able to say that he had never felt fitter in his life and there is no doubt that he then bowled better than at any time in his career. He bowled well in India, was superb against the Australians in 1977 and has since remained a permanent member of the England team.

Derbyshire's Mike Hendrick is another example. He has been troubled quite frequently by strains and injuries over the years – but not since Eddie Barlow became captain at Derbyshire and insisted that the players got and kept themselves really fit.

Eddie did a great job. When he went back to South Africa at the end of 1976 he said, 'Those who want to play for Derbyshire have to get themselves fit this winter. If you are not fit, you don't play. I am not interested in your ability for the time being but I expect you to be fit. If you want to be a pro, act like one.'

He set them a training schedule for the winter months. All their players were given a programme which they had to complete week by week and return to the club secretary. They all buckled down and 1977 was Derbyshire's best season in years – apart from Barlow himself and the New Zealander John Wright they didn't have any new players.

Mike Hendrick kept free from injury, took a lot of wickets during the season and bowled superbly against the Australians. It wasn't coincidence; he was fitter than ever. And it wasn't just a matter of getting fit either. It was a test of character. Would they keep their promise and do their training on cold, frosty nights when Barlow was away? Did they have the discipline and character? They showed they had and

Training is not always a pleasure but it's an important part of the game these days. Hope David Gower manages to keep up . . .!

Modern cricketers seem to spend half their working lives in a tracksuit – jogging, sprinting, stretching. There's not much doubt they are fitter than they have ever been.

Derbyshire as a side was all the better for it. Good professionals.

I mentioned Rod Laver as good example of the professional attitude but the man I consider the complete pro is Jack Nicklaus. A magnificent golfer and a man who has devoted himself to eradicating the smallest weakness in his game.

Luck plays a fair part in sport, there is no doubt about that. But there are too many players who are ready with excuses. 'I was unlucky,' they say. 'That was a great delivery; fancy having to bat against him on this pitch' – there is always something to moan about. The true professional doesn't kid himself. He knows when things are wrong and, more important, he knows why. He doesn't put it all down to luck.

That is what I admire so much about Nicklaus. When the golf season starts in America he never plays in the first tournament; he goes back to the guy who first coached him and spends days doing nothing but hitting hundreds and hundreds of golf balls. Back to basics, thinking about his swing. What can anyone teach a player of Nicklaus' class about golf? But Nicklaus knows that nobody is perfect, he knows that faults creep into your game unnoticed, so he goes back to the beginning, and looks after the details.

At the start of every season and before I go on tour, I visit Johnny Lawrence who has coached me since I was nine years old. He knows my style inside out and we try to go back to basics; there is something he will see which I haven't noticed, like a carpenter who spots a nail that hasn't been driven in straight. It may only be a tiny thing, but it is the small things that get you out; it is only a small thing that makes the difference between 100 or 0, between first and fourth prize. One shot can win or lose the British Open.

Attention to detail and everything which that means – that is the difference between the real professional and the second-rater. If a batsman who gets out can say to himself, 'I shouldn't have stayed out late last night' or 'I shouldn't have had that last drink', 'I should have had a net this morning', 'I should have arrived at the ground thirty minutes earlier' ... he has been unprofessional.

Somebody whom I have never met sent me a beautiful cut-glass goblet after I scored my hundredth hundred in the Test Match at Headingley. It was inscribed 'Genius is infinite patience'. Genuine professionalism costs nothing except time and dedication. Perhaps professionalism is infinite patience plus attention to detail.

2

Building an innings

An innings for most club cricketers begins when they walk out to the wicket and ends – usually sooner rather than later – when they are out. Allowing, of course, for the inquest over a pint after the match when every batsman manages to convince himself he really wasn't out at all. ...

Fair enough. Club cricket is played primarily for enjoyment and there is no call for the intensity of performance demanded by the professional game. But everyone who has held a bat in his hand feels the need to improve himself and I am often asked what are the secrets of building an innings.

Unfortunately there is no magic formula, no mysterious recipe which anyone can pass on. Establishing a major innings is a matter of careful preparation, an eye for detail and complete concentration. It is a determination to learn from every mistake, to cut down the element of chance to the barest possible minimum. Quite simply it is extremely hard work with no absolute guarantee of success.

Wellington is supposed to have said that the Battle of Waterloo was won on the playing fields of Eton and I suppose I have won some of my bigger battles in the front room of a terraced house in Fitzwilliam, because I always begin to plan my strategy the night before a match, to think about the bowlers I am likely to face and to put myself in the right frame of mind for an innings next day.

If a bowler I am due to face has got me out in the past I try to remember how and why, to recall if there was anything exceptional about the dismissal. If there was an unusual reason you can be sure the bowler will have remembered it, so I must be aware of it and try to keep one step ahead. Every bowler has unique characteristics – a good slower ball, a particularly testing yorker and so on; some bowlers are especially dangerous if you try to hit them in certain areas. Factors like these are important and I mull over them the night before a match. It is a great mistake to become anxious and uptight but just as foolish not to be aware of all the possibilities.

I prefer to have breakfast alone on the morning of a match because it helps concentrate my mind. The quieter the better. Similarly, I absolutely hate being rushed when I get to the ground so I have developed a routine – up at a certain time, so much time set aside for travelling to the ground, so much for practice before the match starts. I find that is very important.

The day before I will have decided whether I want a proper net or just a knock-up on the outfield before the match starts. If I want a net I adjust my timing accordingly and arrange for bowlers to be at the ground good and early so we can practise before anyone else arrives. If a knock-up is enough I still get to the ground in good time.

On the first day of a match I always work on the assumption that I will have to bat in the morning. That doesn't always work out, of course, but the important thing is that I am ready just in case. I have lost nothing by being prepared. It is not unusual to wait two days for a knock in a Test Match but in the County Championship you usually have to bat on the first day after a hundred overs. Either way I try to put myself in the right frame of mind so that when I start batting I have done all the groundwork. That, I feel, is vitally important. I do not make a fetish out of studying bowlers or developing a routine which ensures I have time to prepare properly but I do take pains to give myself every chance of success. That is the professional attitude and you see it in other sports besides cricket.

A tournament golfer invariably maps out the course and measures the precise yardage a day or two before he is due to play in an important competition. On the morning of the event he sends out his caddie to plot the exact position of the pin on the green. As little as possible is left to chance.

Top tennis professionals are so evenly matched these days that careful preparation can make all the difference between winning and losing. Jimmy Connors was expected to win the Wimbledon final in 1975 but he was beaten by Arthur Ashe – and Ashe said afterwards it was because he had planned how to win some time before the match took place. Ashe thought back over his meetings with Connors and realized that the tactics he employed then just didn't work so he changed his game, brought Connors into the net and beat him. That's how decisive good preparation can be.

Pre-match practice takes into account the sort of bowlers you expect to meet during the innings. Naturally, you rate some bowlers more highly than others and expect to score off one man, accept that you will have to be very watchful against another. Every bowling attack has its relative weakness and it is up to the batsman to spot it and try to take advantage of it.

A quick look at the pitch is important. How much grass is there? Will the ball seam or turn, how high is it likely to bounce? Does the pitch have any special characteristics which ought to be borne in mind? Some pitches do play lower than others and there is not much point remembering that after you have played back in the first over and been trapped lbw. Others may profit from your mistake and play forward happily all day, but that is not much consolation.

Considerations like these can be taken into account before a batsman actually faces a delivery and may well save him during the most difficult part of the innings – the first few overs. Every batsman is at his most vulnerable then and every plan and precaution I have mentioned is aimed at helping me through the testing overs against the new ball. I want to be as ready as possible for anything that might happen and I certainly do not want to be surprised by something I ought to have foreseen.

The state of the game will naturally have a bearing on the way you approach an

Laird dropped by Brearley off the bowling of Botham – but the non-striker can't relax. Concentration is a habit which has to be developed through conscious practice.

innings. If I have to score quickly I try to work out a positive method of doing so rather than going in with some general notion of 'getting on with it'. That way you avoid the tension which so often helps to get a batsman out.

It is not possible to plan an innings in great detail from the outset because there are too many unknown factors. But if there is a target to achieve – a possible declaration or so many runs for victory – it makes sense to work out how many runs you ought to score in a session. Cricket has become a bit preoccupied with overs and there is a tendency to think in terms of so many runs per over to achieve objectives; I think it is much more sensible to think in terms of time. That way I am prepared for a bowler to have an exceptional spell during which it is virtually impossible to get him away. I don't start to worry if he bowls tightly and the going is tough for half an hour, there is still another thirty minutes to make up the leeway.

I try to plan over a period of time and the longer the better. If you have four hours to bat for victory it is nonsense to think in terms of four runs an over ... that creates more problems than it solves. How many runs should you have after two hours, how many after tea, how many can you score in the last session – that is a more realistic approach. I accept this is a philosophy geared to Test Match and Championship cricket but that is basically my game. I confess that the form of cricket I find especially difficult is forty-over stuff which is so often reduced to a quick slog for runs. A fast thirty and out is not my way of playing the game; I am a big score man, basically one of the old school.

Because I bat for long periods people often ask me how I relax in the middle. The answer is simple enough – I don't. The secret is to stay mentally keyed-up and alert all the time, physically loose but mentally wound-up. Some of my worst performances have been the result of feeling too tense physically and I guard against that, but mental tension is vital because without it there is no concentration.

Unlike a lot of players I concentrate as hard at the non-striker's end as I do when I am facing. It is easy to imagine that because you are not actually facing your wicket is in no danger. Some players relax consciously at the non-striker's end: their eyes are open but they are not really seeing everything that's going on. That is dangerous, the root cause behind any number of run outs, because one player's concentration does not match a situation which develops with dramatic suddenness.

Take golf again. Jack Nicklaus plays four or five hours in a major tournament round and he concentrates completely all the time, not just when he is playing the ball. You never see Nicklaus waving to the crowd down the fairway or admiring the birds in the trees; he talks to his caddie about the next shot, concentrates entirely on the job in hand. And there is precious little frivolity between sets in a top tennis match; players use every available minute to key themselves up for the next game, the next rally. Concentration like that is absolutely vital on a cricket field.

Concentration enables a batsman to sense when he is becoming careless – and that can happen to the best of players during a long innings. The danger signs may be small enough but they have to be recognized. If I play and miss, for instance, I want to know why and I run through the possible causes in my mind as quickly as I can. If it was an exceptional delivery, fair enough, but if I can honestly think of no good reason for the mistake I make a conscious effort to intensify my concentration.

'Think about it; you didn't get your foot over enough; play a bit straighter; you played outside to it then; don't get clever; play it simply' – those are the kind of things I tell myself. Only the best is good enough and I get very angry with myself if the standard slips.

Being totally aware of what's going on in the middle also helps you to sense when you have a bowler where you want him. It doesn't happen often – certainly not often enough – but when you are playing really well you can feel if a bowler is getting desperate. He cannot get you out and he knows it; worse from his point of view he knows that you know it as well. But he cannot hide, he cannot escape. He has to go on bowling in a sort of limbo, knowing full well that no matter what he does you have a counter for him. When you know you have made a bowler accept your superiority it is a marvellous feeling of accomplishment.

There was a time when the only man I talked to during an innings was me. Chatter out in the middle used to upset me badly; I was so cocooned in my innings that I didn't want to talk to anybody in case it upset my concentration.

I am still not a great one for idle chat when I am batting but it doesn't upset me any more. Perhaps that is because I have learned to relax, grown up over the years, gained more experience. Now I accept that it is important to establish a rapport between batsmen, especially in Test Matches, because you have to work as a team, help and encourage each other. I like to keep the talk down to a minimum and strictly to the point but I realize how helpful it can be.

I always work on the assumption that it is we two against the other thirteen – and I include the umpires not as a slight on their impartiality but because you have to consider the longest possible odds. The batsmen are out on their own and they have to lean on each other when they can.

Sometimes I will ask my partner how I look from his end. Am I playing straight, what did that one do when I played and missed just now? He is in a good position to spot details and as I have already said it is easy for errors to creep in unnoticed when you get tired. Similarly, I try to tip him the wink if it looks as though he isn't aware of a mistake he is making.

If you make a mistake and are lucky enough to get away with it you should take advantage of it. There is little enough room for error, so the quicker you are made aware of faults the quicker you can put them right and your batting partner helps a lot. A smile or a knowing look is about as close as I like to come to frivolity. But it is useful and important to discuss the pacing of an innings, where you might take a quick single, whether a fielder is changing position and so on. All useful just as long as it does not affect a batsman's concentration. It is not a debating society and I don't have much time for idle chatter.

Crowd reaction rarely bothers me. However, it is a tremendous boost to feel the crowd are on your side, like the day at Headingley when I scored my hundredth century in a Test Match against Australia; I felt then that people were willing me to succeed and they may never realize just how much they helped.

I tend to play better under pressure, when I feel it is absolutely vital to do well and I wanted to repay a lot of faith that day. Similarly, if players try to put me under pressure by swearing or telling me I'm no good it makes me all the more determined to prove them wrong.

Events off the field do not disturb me in the slightest. At Lahore in the winter of 1976 during the First Test there was a crowd disturbance which eventually developed into a full-blown riot but I would have been happy to bat on. I can cut myself off from the crowd, from anything else that might be going on round the ground and concentrate entirely on the job in hand. Naturally I am aware of noise and atmosphere, aware that something is happening when there is crowd trouble on any scale but basically there might be two men and a dog out there and I would still play with the same basic requirements in mind.

Anything which forces a batsman to break his concentration is potentially dangerous, so I am very wary of relaxing during breaks for drinks, brief as they are, in Test Matches. Wickets tend to fall soon after intervals simply because batsmen have switched off and cannot switch on again quickly enough. I try to remember that I am still batting and that the pressure will be on again in a few minutes.

Longer intervals like lunch and tea require a slightly different approach, depending on whether I have been playing well or badly. If I am happy with my performance I like to switch off completely, strip down and relax. There is no point in going over what has happened, recalling a good shot or re-living anything in the previous session: that is history. I am more interested in what is likely to happen when I go in again.

Five or ten minutes before play is due to resume I begin to switch on again, run through their likely plan of attack in my mind and if there is a target to chase or a declaration to aim for, give some thought to what my battle plan must be. While things are going well there is no need for inquests.

If I am not happy with the way things are going I use the intervals very differently. Experienced players can often see things from the boundary edge which are not obvious in the middle so I sound out one or two of the lads and ask them if they can offer some explanation why I am not going well. Knowing what is wrong is half the battle and by the time I have added their suggestions to a few ideas of my own I usually come up with a pretty clear picture of what is needed. Then, and only then, I can relax a bit, happier in my mind that I know how to put my game right.

Eventually every batsman gets out and there has been a fair amount of codswallop talked in the past about my attitude in the dressing-room. Apparently I throw bats about and tear pads off in a rage ... rubbish! Quite apart from anything else I value my kit far too much to start slinging it around; I take a lot of time and pains to see my equipment is just right and I never remember throwing it around in a dressing-room.

I sit down quietly and think about how I got out – was it a poor shot, a good delivery, a lapse in concentration? It is worth a bit of thought. When I first started

The poster is not very complimentary and Rodney Hogg seems to know whose funeral it ought to be! Concentration is absolutely vital in situations like this.

the inquest used to take ages, I used to spend literally hours turning it over in my mind. I felt a real failure just because I had got out.

That's gone now. I usually ask a couple of questions in the dressing-room and later I may seek out an umpire to ask exactly where a delivery pitched and what it did because he is in the perfect position to see. Once I know exactly why I got out I can take steps to see it doesn't happen again. ...

3

All change

One of the most common criticisms levelled against cricket is that it refuses to change. The game always stands accused of being a generation out of date, dragging its feet while other sports develop quickly to take advantage of the latest fashion. Lord's is a cartoonist's dream, represented as being full of Colonel Blimps with ideas set firmly against progress.

I certainly do not think all the right decisions have been made in cricket during the many years since I first played for Yorkshire, but there is no doubt that the game has accepted change. The format of the game is vastly different today from the one I first encountered. The first sponsored competition, the Gillette Cup, was on the horizon, but the game was dominated by three-day championship cricket. Players developed a routine knowing that they would play six days a week and have a day off on Sunday.

Saturday nights were very different then. Teams used to relax, throw themselves a party of sorts, have a late night in the knowledge that they could sleep in the next day. And Sunday was a day for playing golf if you were away from home, for relaxing with the family during home matches. We even had Sunday lunch in those days. ...

It was a pleasant, ordered lifestyle and more than that, it helped players with their game because they knew just what was expected of them. They played the same sort of cricket week in week out, they could assess how much batting or bowling they would have to do, they developed the rhythm which is so vitally important in first-class cricket.

Rothmans eventually pioneered a one-day team, the Cavaliers, who played on Sundays in what amounted to exhibition matches. Many top players were invited to take part; former stars like Evans, Compton and Laker came out of retirement to add novelty to the matches. It was a good vehicle for the sponsors and it helped beneficiaries. But nobody really imagined then that they were about to start a revolution in the game.

Counties saw how good the one-day attendances were and naturally wanted to cash in if they could. Several experimented with championship cricket on Sundays, and the gates suggested it could be made a success. Sunday attendances tended to be slightly higher than Saturday even allowing for the inconvenience of having to buy a programme for admission to fit in with the Sunday Observance laws.

23

Yorkshire never tried Sunday Championship cricket then, and I think they made a big mistake. They were suspicious of innovation and conservative when they really needed foresight and courage to give Sunday play a trial. Such is their status in the game that they might have given cricket a lead; I feel sure that Yorkshire supporters, steeped as they are in the tradition of three-day cricket, would have shown that Sunday Championship cricket could be made to work profitably. Instead, John Player stepped in with what seemed like a big-money offer then and the counties opted for a limited-overs competition. It was not riches by any means, but it was available without much effort on the part of the county administrators. Sunday Championship cricket was shelved and the forty-over Sunday league was born.

I still believe that if counties had experimented with championship cricket on Sundays for, say, three years they would have benefited at least as much as they have under the present format. Financially they might not have done quite as well, though I see no reason to suppose they could not have sold Sunday Championship cricket to TV as lucratively as they did the limited-overs game. But at least the accent would have stayed on proper cricket – and only that produces Test Match players.

Championship matches on Sunday would have helped keep the public educated in favour of real cricket. There is now such a surfeit of one-day – and the sixteen-match Sunday league comprises much of it – that spectators have come to admire and accept slog cricket to the detriment of the three-day game. They have set standards by it. I know that the Sunday league has provided financial benefits over the years and I do not underestimate the importance of that. But if it has educated the public against what I call proper cricket then it has been a failure; nothing it has put into the game can compensate for that.

When I first entered county cricket it was dominated by fine English players, such as Dexter, Cowdrey, Barrington, Graveney, Edrich and many more. By the late sixties overseas players were appearing in growing numbers; now their impact on the English game is almost overwhelming. Counties measure their strength on the ability of the overseas players in their team. Gloucestershire became Proctershire, Lancashire-Lloydshire, Warwickshire became Westindieshire. When we at Yorkshire think of a rival county we think in terms of overseas players; how many runs will he get, how many wickets will so-and-so take. Almost invariably the chief danger is posed by an overseas star.

The temptation to recruit overseas players was understandable, and most counties fell for it with mindless speed. The call for new-look cricket which produced limited-overs competitions also created a rush to sign overseas stars. Once one County did it the others were afraid of being left behind. Many Counties saw overseas players as a ready-made way to plug gaps in their team. It was quick, relatively easy and less costly than producing good English players of their own.

The alternative is a slow and uncertain business, as Yorkshire know only too well. A youngster has to be retrained for several years while he is learning his trade on the ground staff, in the Second XI, during the formative years when he is not quite good enough for a first team place. When he does make the first team it is likely to take him at least three years to establish himself and begin to repay the time and trouble which the county has taken. Five or six years of patience and expense and you have – hooray – one English player. It takes five minutes to sign a player from overseas.

All the counties – except Yorkshire – opted for the cheap and quick alternative to producing their own players. And you could hardly blame the players themselves for accepting lucrative offers; it was money far beyond most of them could hope to earn in their own countries. As professionals they saw a great career opportunity and took it with both hands.

So overseas players dominated the thinking of many counties and the attention of most spectators. And while they were receiving publicity and praise, the young English players in the team were half forgotten, their opportunities to shine and increase their confidence eroded by the presence of bigger names. English youngsters developed inferiority complexes, and no wonder.

Television – the third major change on the County cricket scene since I started – did not help their particular problem. I am not blaming TV for that. It is a marvellous medium which has taken the game into the homes of many who might never have watched a match, and it quite naturally seeks to reflect what interests people most. But TV concentrated on the glamour of the overseas star rather than on the potential of young English players.

Listen to the commentator on a televised cricket match and the chances are he will be talking about the overseas players involved. This is natural enough, since they tend to be the better players and dominate the course of matches. But I still think it is a pity that more publicity has not been given to young English players; TV so often gives the impression that overseas stars are the only men on the field.

Publicity of the right type is important for a young player. Everybody likes to be given credit for doing well, and TV can help speed up a youngster's development by giving him pride in his achievements and the confidence that goes with it. In Australia, where home-bred players have not had to compete with overseas stars to anything like the same extent, a young man who does well in a match on TV can become a celebrity overnight. Australian TV is not coy about praising its sports stars either. Men like Lillee and Thomson are national heroes, their status is unchallenged, and that does a tremendous amount for their self-confidence. In England we seem to want to put our best players in their place; in Australia they put them on a pedestal.

I am not knocking British television, because it does cricket a great service and, after all, it only mirrors the game which the administrators have produced. But it does help to illustrate what a dominant position overseas stars enjoy in the English game.

The effect of limited-overs cricket, overseas players and the publicity which surrounds both is difficult to assess because it is felt on two fronts. On one hand there are business considerations, and cricket, like any other business, has to pay its way. On the other, there is the development of the game as a game. And what is good for one need not necessarily be good for the other.

Sunday cricket, the most restricted of the limited-overs competitions, can rightly claim to attract spectators who might otherwise see no cricket at all. My mother used to watch it on TV every week and quite enjoyed it. But I still have to be convinced that my mother watching TV on a Sunday afternoon really did anything for the game of cricket. It shows an interest, of course, and that is important for the future, but the game of cricket does not derive a great deal from TV ratings. John Player matches attract good crowds but, as I have already said, I think there would have been just as much interest in Championship cricket played on Sundays and properly projected by TV. And I feel it is easy to overstate the financial benefits of TV coverage; considering that the cash has to be split among seventeen counties I think TV gets Sunday cricket on the cheap.

A limited-overs competition provides a day out for the family, a form of cricket which people only mildly interested in the three-day game might take to and enjoy. And there is no doubt that cricket has benefited from higher standards of fielding and running between the wickets. But there are very serious disadvantages which have to be taken into account. Limited-overs cricket has helped produce bowlers whose qualities – if you can call them that – are almost entirely defensive. I wouldn't call myself a very good bowler but even I can bowl a few good overs. A breed of medium-pacers who are negative in their attitude because they know the rules of the competitions do not demand that they should actually bowl anybody out. A wicket is a bonus, but a maiden over can be just as valuable. Hardly the kind of attitude or aptitude likely to win Test Matches.

Because it favours negative thinking, limited-overs cricket puts the onus entirely on batsmen. The fielding side have only to absorb a certain amount of deliveries and the lower the final score the more satisfied they are. So it's all up to the batsman, and he has to contend with defensive field placing, defensive tactics perfected by captains who meet the same situation week after week.

It may have helped some batsmen marginally by forcing them to go out and hit the ball hard. Players who lacked confidence in their ability have discovered that they can score quickly; it has brought them out of their defensive shell and made them rather more rounded performers. But that is a fringe benefit which applies only to the few. Generally, one-day cricket has produced a breed of sloggers and moderate itsy-bitsy players who enjoy a brief sort of stardom once a week. A quick thirty with the bat, two for twenty with the ball, and a player has won the Man of the Match Award when in fact what he did was to slog three fours and a six, get out entertainingly and then block up an end with the help of a defensive field. On the strength of that he is a 'good player'.

I always enjoyed captaining one-day cricket because it made exceptional demands on experience and speed of thought. Everything happens quickly and captaincy in those circumstances can become a real challenge. But it certainly does nothing to produce players of lasting quality, and that is a sadness and a sickness in the modern game reflected by the abundance of moderate players and the worrying shortage of Test material.

How can a batsman hope to learn his trade on Sunday afternoon? He angles the ball to third man through a non-existent slip and it is accepted as a legitimate stroke. The same shot a day later loses him his wicket. Terrible shot that. Play a straight shot in one-day cricket and everyone bawls for you to get on with it, give it a slog. You are forced to play exactly the kind of shot which guarantees your downfall in a Test Match.

I cannot help thinking there was more than an element of limited-overs influence in England's performance against Lillee and Thomson in Australia in 1974–5. Hardly anyone got behind the line of the ball, batsmen were trying to glance and steer instead of playing straight. Don't blame the batsmen for that; blame the system which forces them to slog at least once a week during their working lives.

We have plenty of players who can score a bright, breezy little thirty, the sort of innings which is just right for limited-overs games, but that sort of player will not win us Test Matches. We need batsmen who can make correct fifties and eighties and occasional centuries.

When I look at the effect which limited-overs cricket is having on the game I can understand the reaction of players of the older generation, men like Brian Close, who learned their business in the three-day game. Closey saw all the disadvantages long before most people suspected what might happen, but when he spoke out he was accused of being unnecessarily anti.

Well, I am not against one-day cricket as such but I cannot condone many of its effects on the game in the middle. How ironic that a form of cricket introduced with the promise of producing carefree, positive entertainment should have become the most negative of games to play. Certainly it provides a spectacle, but whether that spectacle is cricket is another matter.

One unfortunate and important result of one-day matches is that players are now involved in more travelling than ever before. Compared with the early sixties, weekends these days are a calamity. It is not unusual for a team to travel 150 miles on a Friday night after a Championship match, book in at a hotel, play Saturday and then book out to travel on for a Sunday league match. Book into a new hotel on Saturday night, book out on Sunday morning, play the match and then motor back to the hotel they left the previous day. No wonder we are pretty expert at packing clothes and kit these days – and no wonder many players are exhausted by the start of the week.

Players have often asked that Sunday fixtures should be arranged to avoid unnecessary travelling, but there seems to be a belief that gates suffer when the same sides meet in championship and Sunday matches over a weekend. Well, figures do not bear that out. But it seems we shall continue to hare up and down motorways at weekends until something happens to jolt the administration into making a change. I am afraid that that something may just be a tired cricketer killed in a road accident.

The fashion for importing overseas stars had a striking effect on England's Test performances against other countries, especially West Indies and Pakistan until the advent of WSC. When I first played Test cricket in 1964 England could hold her own against most countries, especially in England, but this has been eroded over the years.

We used to have two important advantages at home over teams like West Indies and Pakistan, both of which have been frittered away since overseas players came into the game. First, we were accustomed to playing on our surfaces, which are unlike any other in the world. And secondly, we tended to fight harder when the chips were down – and that is not just a fanciful bit of sabre-rattling. It has been proved on many occasions.

Naturally enough, once overseas players became part of the English game their County team-mates wanted them to do well for the side. So they passed on tips, expert advice, experience of how to play such and such a bowler and how to treat this pitch and that pitch. Gradually overseas players became more accustomed to pitches which seamed and turned. And the same overseas players learned slowly but surely how to fight their way out of a difficult situation – it was expected of them. Their team-mates would lift them when they were down, and the ability to overcome problems with technique and patience when necessary became part of their everyday cricket life. They already had plenty of flair, and playing in English conditions helped round off their game.

Inevitably, when they met England in Test Matches they were much harder nuts to crack, not just in their own countries but over here as well. We had educated them to beat us. The West Indies team which beat England at Lord's in 1973 was full of players who had considerable experience of English conditions through their contracts with County sides. They did not have an exceptionally formidable trio of fast bowlers as they did three years later, but they did have flair and invaluable knowledge of English conditions. They had learned their lessons well.

Steps are being taken to limit the number of overseas players in County sides, and that must be a good thing from England's point of view. There is no doubt that the number and quality of English players coming along has dropped since overseas players were accepted into the County game, and cricket's administrators must take their share of the blame for that. Those who decried the performance of the England side in 1974–6 before WSC came on the scene and who even now moan about the standard of English players are often the same men who are filling their County sides with as many overseas players as possible so they can bask in local success. They are hypocrites. If they want to buy success for their Counties and enjoy the glory that brings, they should keep quiet and accept a second-rate national side. After all, they did much to create it.

During my absence from the England team I know many committee men from other Counties were happy to blame me for the defeats of 1974 and afterwards. And having had their say they went back to Counties full of overseas players. What the hell do they think they were doing about England's problems, about the fact that the selectors are hamstrung because so many important County places are taken by players who are ineligible for England?

Yorkshire would win something next season if they imported two overseas stars.

There is nothing to prevent them doing so, no rule against it apart from an unwritten one which I hope will never be broken. But the principle is important as far as Yorkshire are concerned. Theirs is not the easiest way, and they have suffered for it in terms of trophies, but the easiest way is not always the best way for English cricket.

The modern game is a far more demanding one than it was fifteen years ago. Not more competitive – the Championship was always fiercely contested – but definitely sharper. There is a cut-throat air about limited-overs matches, often played before good crowds who cheer or moan with every run. No draw, no reasonable pace: a modern player is under far more pressure than he was when I started.

Unfortunately cricket seems to have fallen into a trap familiar in sport – the belief that winning is all important and the guy who comes second is a failure. Third place is not regarded as a great achievement. Nobody is really concerned whether a side has battled against injuries or whether the season has produced valuable pointers to the future. Win or lose, succeed or fail ... and the players are caught up in the middle of it, constantly aware that they are under pressure to win something.

It has become impossible to do well and lose. Soon after a narrow defeat people will slap you on the back and say hard luck, well played, never mind. Three weeks later they are complaining because the side has had a bad season.

Mid-July is the anxious time. By then, most clubs have gone out of the Benson and Hedges Cup, perhaps they are half-way down the Sunday league, half-way in the Championship. The Gillette Cup represents the last chance of winning something, and the pressure is really on. Lose in the Gillette and the recriminations start: this player is not good enough, that player will have to go; the captaincy comes under fire. More competitions provide more chance of winning a trophy, but they also mean more sides are accused of failure. Clubs are naturally anxious about the financial future; loss of revenue from cup ties provides the flashpoint for all sorts of arguments and irrational reactions.

Fear of failure, the pressure applied often unwittingly by the media, County clubs and spectators has led to an increase in gamesmanship over the years. I have noticed it creeping stealthily into the game, and from what I hear at cricket meetings the authorities are concerned about it too. Umpires complain that their job has become harder than ever. Tension and pressure bring irritation, nerve-endings get a bit frayed. More and more matches become needle matches until players who are basically sportsmen do something on the spur of the moment they will regret a few hours later. They go over the edge, just for a moment, and spoil a reputation for fair play which is generally deserved.

4

Past masters

Sport lends itself to all sorts of arguments as to who were the greatest players, the biggest personalities, and which were the best teams of all time. There is an endless fascination in speculating whether Muhammad Ali would have beaten Rocky Marciano, whether Stanley Matthews would have been as formidable a player in modern football, whether many of the great teams of the past would have beaten the best in the game today.

Great names in cricket fascinate me because as a professional I always want to compare my performance with the best. There are any number of past cricketers whom I would love to have seen simply because they are acknowledged as the masters, batsmen I would like to have played alongside and bowlers I regret never having faced. Their reputations have become a fundamental part of the game's history and I would love to have seen many of them at first hand.

Three batsmen spring instantly to mind in that respect – Hutton, Compton and the incomparable Bradman. I never saw any of them play.

That may come as a surprise in the case of Hutton, if only because so many people have commented on the similarities of our style. It seems to have become accepted that I modelled myself on Hutton, and that simply is not so; I never saw him play a first-class innings and in fact I never met him until I had played a year or so in County cricket.

The nearest I came to seeing him for Yorkshire was when I went with the secretary of my local Ackworth club to Bradford in the fifties. It rained and we never saw a ball bowled. Many years later I played in a benefit match for Jimmy Binks at Hull and Hutton played on the other side; I remember I asked if I could field at short leg – hardly my position – so I could watch how he used his feet.

As the bowler delivered the ball Hutton tended to play half forward. His left foot went down the pitch about a foot or eighteen inches and then he continued forward into his stroke or balanced on to his back foot. Now that was fascinating considering our styles were supposed to be so similar because my initial movement is quite the opposite – slightly back and across. Both initial movements are only slight, of course, but it is odd that we should be regarded as being so alike when in fact our basic initial movements were so different.

Len Hutton would be a
fine model for any batsman
– but I never saw him play
a first-class innings.

Denis Compton – an
unpredictable genius but
perhaps more orthodox
than his reputation
suggests.

Yet so many players who saw Hutton tell me they see a lot of him in the way I play. Perhaps we have characteristics in common – determination, concentration, patience, a correct basic technique. Alan Davidson says he is struck by the similarity in our make-up and general style of play and Clyde Walcott would not believe me when I told him I had never had a chance to study Hutton's style.

Whatever similarities there are happened either by accident or perhaps were created by the environment we were both brought up in, playing for Yorkshire on surfaces which encouraged a particular style of play. The idea that I consciously modelled myself on him is a fallacy.

Hutton will probably be remembered best for that marvellous cover-drive. They say he liked the ball going away from him so he could lean into it and play that fabulous caress of a stroke through the covers. Because I play back initially my best shot is probably a cover-drive from a ball just short of a length; I don't even know how I do it but I have been able to play it naturally from an early age.

In the Test Match at Hyderabad in January 1968 I played one shot I will remember for a long time, letting a widish delivery come right on and then playing it in a huge arc through the covers for four. 'Just like Leonard, that,' I thought as I hit it. That thought alone made my afternoon.

Denis Compton has been described as an unpredictable genius and there is certainly something of both in his record. Any man who could reach the heights of 1947, when he scored eighteen centuries and over 3,000 runs, has more than a touch of genius in him; his unpredictability became a watchword, almost the trademark, of his career.

I would like to have seen Compo play because I have heard so much about his sweep, how he used to go down the pitch even to medium-pacers, how he did all kinds of extraordinary things at the crease. I would like to have seen it for myself because I don't entirely believe it.

Don't misunderstand me. I am sure that Compton was unorthodox, unusually inventive, delightful to watch when he was in form and happy to play shots which struck spectators as dashing and cheeky. One of the beauties of cricket is the fact that people remember one or two special things from a day's play; legends grow around them in the bar and during the long winter months. By the time they have been told and retold a hundred times a batsman finds he has been playing a particular shot in every innings all through the season when in fact he played it once or twice.

Yorkshire's Mel Ryan recalls how he was running in against Compton with the new ball and got as far as his delivery stride when he realized Compton was three yards down the pitch to meet him. Too late to do anything about it, too surprised to change his mind and Compton belted the delivery many a mile. The point is that that is what Ryan remembers above all else about Compton – one extraordinary shot. That is how legends are made.

I have spoken to several old cricketers whose knowledge I respect, men who have watched Compton bat with a professional eye rather than from the understandably coloured viewpoint of a spectator. And they say that Compton was quite orthodox in many of his shots, that his bat was as straight as anybody's and his feet were properly positioned more often than not. I am not saying he was not a master of the unexpected but I do distrust the belief that nothing he did came out of the coaching manual. He was not all improvisation.

What he undoubtedly must have had was a marvellous eye. A bowler might think he had beaten him but the bat would arrive at the very latest moment. Compton would fall into his shot and the ball would skittle away for a couple of runs. Always ready to attack and a wonderful sweeper and cutter, he must have been someone worth watching. But I still think there was more of the technician in him than he is given credit for or his reputation would have us believe; there are some basics common to all great batsmen whatever their idiosyncrasies or favourite shots.

If Leonard Hutton was the technical perfectionist and Denis Compton the great entertainer of his day, Don Bradman was surely the nearest thing to a run machine cricket has ever seen. A player apart, a man twenty years before his time.

Facts and figures insist he was a phenomenon and nobody would ever dream of challenging his status in world cricket. What fascinates me about the man is the way he scored his runs so quickly and so consistently ... I confess I find it extraordinary that his opponents did not – could not – find a way of restricting him. Of all batsmen I would like to have seen Bradman because I would like to know for myself just how far ahead of his contemporaries he was. More than that, I should like to know why.

I can appreciate that he was a phenomenal player and an amazing runmaker. What I find difficult to fathom is how, for instance, he could score 300 runs in a day at Headingley – because the immediate reaction of the fielding side nowadays would be to go on the defensive, feed the freescoring batsman singles and aim to bowl at his weaker partner.

When Bradman played at Headingley England bowled nearly 130 overs in the day; when I scored my hundredth century there against Australia they bowled 87. Simple mathematics suggests a batsman should score more runs if he faces more overs but Bradman made three times as many as I did and didn't receive anything like three times the number of overs. I find that kind of mathematics quite staggering and I should love to have seen the sort of bowling he faced and the sort of fields which were set to him.

Bill Bowes tells me they had an idea that if they bowled on or just outside off stump and swung the ball away, Bradman must eventually get an edge. So they put in three slips and two gullies – and he hit the bowling mercilessly through the covers. And that went on virtually all day, except that England put an extra man in the mid-off cover area and Bradman varied his attack by using his famous pull through mid-wicket against anything short.

That could never happen today. Part of me says it was a foolish way to counter a batsman of his ability and another part accepts that these were experienced, intelligent cricketers who simply could not keep him quiet.

That's the magic of Bradman. The more you read about him the more you wish you had actually seen the man and tried to work him out for yourself. Either he was

The incomparable Don Bradman. How on earth could any batsman score three hundred runs in a day . . .?

years ahead of his appreciation of the game or the tactics employed against him left a lot to be desired. And I would be the last person to minimize his ability; you simply have to accept that he was a phenomenon by any standards.

I first met Bradman in Australia and was fortunate enough to spend some time in conversation with him – not enough, I might say, because there were always so many people around wanting a little of his time. It was obvious that he had – and has – a brilliant cricket brain. And much as he is justifiably proud of what he has achieved he is a very practical and honest man.

In the mid-sixties he was asked how many runs he thought he might score in a six-hour Test day under current conditions and he said: 'I think I would be lucky if I got 200 once in a while; I think it would be somewhere around 170.' Project that forward more than ten years to the present day, when over-rates are much lower and fields are more defensive and it seems clear that his expectation would fall well below 170 now. Obviously Bradman accepted that fact and I respected him for it; many older players are fond of claiming they would have got even more runs and wickets in the modern game. And Bradman was not just being modest. He has a well-developed awareness of his status in the game and rightly so. When he admitted he might not have scored as many runs in modern cricket he was simply being frank and that was something which all the players present noticed and respected at the time.

Another aspect of Bradman's career which always fascinated me was the way he captivated the Australian nation. Older Australian players tell me how people used to ring the ground to ask if he was batting and if he was in at lunch they would flock to the game expecting to see him make a double hundred. When he got out, they went home.

That sounds like a benefit match on a huge scale, the sort of situation where crowds turn out to see the local favourite and then drift away when he is out. The man had become bigger than the game itself. I find that very hard to grasp but if it is true – and I am sure it is – then he was not only a staggering player but a man with staggering appeal.

As a professional I would like to have been able to study Bradman with a professional's eye. No doubt many modern cricket followers would like the opportunity to watch him at his best for the sheer pleasure of the spectacle. I would study him, try to dissect him, discover how and why he made the impact he did. Any man as exceptional as Bradman is an intriguing figure to his fellow-professionals; no doubt seeing would have been believing everything about him.

As a batsman myself there are obviously certain bowlers I would like to have seen and faced – out of curiosity and professional pride. There are so many great bowlers in the history of the game but I would particularly like to have had a go against Statham and Trueman and especially Fred.

I played against Statham in the early sixties and got some inkling of how fine a bowler he was but naturally I never played serious cricket against Fred at his best. And I think that would have been a bit special.

35

Fred says he was the best and that's good enough for me. Even if he did threaten to knock my head off . . .

If I am asked which fast bowler I rate most highly I usually say, 'Fred says it was Fred and I'm not going to argue with him.' I have the greatest admiration and respect for him.

Back in 1968 when I was recovering from a back injury which had put me out of the game for almost two months I joined Fred on an end-of-season tour of Devon and Cornwall. 'You come with me, I'll look after you, Sunshine,' he said.

I travelled with him, roomed with him, ate with him and then one day we were put on opposite sides in a match. ...

The third delivery from Fred, an outswinging yorker, hit me right on the toe and I went down like a sack of potatoes. Half aware that Fred was leaping about appealing for lbw I shouted, 'I hit it, Fred, I hit it.'

And my soul-mate of the last five days shouted back, 'Hit it? It ought to have knocked your bloody rotten head off.'

Not bad for a bloke who started the tour promising to look after 'Sunshine'.

He was a great help to me in my early days with Yorkshire, always encouraging me, watching me bat. I used to have him on, telling him he wasn't really fast while the rest of the team rolled their eyes and Fred looked as though he didn't quite know whether to take this young upstart seriously or not. 'I'll get you, Sunshine, just you wait,' he promised.

The indoor nets at Headingley were out of commission so we had to have pre-season practice outdoors at Bradford, where the pitches tend to be damp and can be a bit awkward in April. Fred was bowling at a nice steady pace until I got into his net, then he came charging in, hit me on the hand, knocked a couple of knuckles off ... it didn't take me long to decide I'd had enough of that.

'See,' crowed Fred, 'I told you I'd get you, you four-eyed failure.'

He hadn't forgotten – but then Fred forgot very little in his life. He has a wonderfully retentive memory which is one reason why he is in such demand as an after-dinner speaker these days.

Fred is a remarkable person, a man from mining stock like me who was determined to succeed and worked his way right to the top of his profession. And he is the only sportsman I know who is instantly identified just by his Christian name. Fred is Fred to every sports fan in the world – and that in itself is an amazing achievement.

It may sound a little like a death wish but I would like to have had a go against Lindwall and Miller – if only because their 1948 Australian side was reputed to be one of the strongest ever. Everyone knows how that team destroyed England and Hutton himself recalls what a torrid time Lindwall and Miller gave the best of the English batsmen.

I have met them both which makes them even more intriguing. Miller is flamboyant, extrovert, 'Nugget' to his friends, unpredictable and aggressive on the field. Lindwall is built like Fred – strong and chunky with a powerful neck and backside. I am sure that playing against them would not have been a pleasant experience but I would have liked a go just for the hell of it.

Ray Lindwall (*left*) and Keith Miller – facing them can't have been a pleasant experience but I would have liked a go.

Tony Lock (*left*) and Jim Laker – Yorkshire had plenty of respect for these two; Where on earth is the next run coming from?

The fact that they are Australian makes them all the more interesting. There have been some great fast bowling partnerships – Adcock and Heine for South Africa, Hall and Griffith for West Indies – but there seems so much more to play for in an Ashes series for any English batsman, so Lindwall and Miller mean something special to me.

Lock and Laker on a turning English pitch is a challenge which I might not have actually enjoyed but one which I am sure I would have found absorbing, to say the least. Yorkshire and Surrey battled for the championship during the fifties and although Yorkshire's team was good enough to win it in any other era, Surrey just had the edge. Lock and Laker had a lot to do with that.

When I first made the side in 1962, Yorkshire's players had plenty of respect for the Surrey pair. They said playing against them was a bit of a nightmare, that Laker was a marvellous loop bowler and the only way to score off him was to have a slog from time to time; they recognized a craftsman when they met one.

Ray Illingworth said the Lock bowling on a turner was virtually impossible to get away – he pushed the ball through so quickly and turned it so sharply that batsmen despaired of getting down the wicket to him. Survival was difficult enough. When I asked Illy where batsmen scored runs against him he said simply – they didn't.

There was a possibility that I might have got runs with my back-foot shot against the ball going away from just short of a length, through the covers because there were bound to be men in close catching positions. But really, it seems that life against Lock and Laker on a turning pitch was as near impossible for batsmen as made no difference. Batsmen needed real technique just to survive and give themselves half a chance to make a few runs – and that is the sort of situation which appeals to me.

Ramadhin and Valentine will always have a special place in Test Match history and affection. Valentine, rather overshadowed by his partner, was a marvellous foil and a very accurate bowler who spun the ball a great deal by all accounts.

I doubt if anyone ever really worked out Ramadhin but May and Cowdrey exploded the myth of his near-invincibility at Birmingham in 1957, largely by employing pad-play against him. It was a relatively new idea, not pretty to watch but resourceful and successful and it caught on throughout County cricket. Now it is regarded as a necessary evil in the game, used by players to survive as pitches have become more helpful to bowlers. Many players today leave the bat behind the pad, not really trying to play the ball but making a pretence of doing so to avoid being given out lbw without offering a stroke.

As more and more players employed their pads against Ramadhin he became frustrated and disillusioned. Having been brought up in the West Indies where batsmen play at the ball it was not his idea of how the game should be played. When I bumped into him on a few occasions against Lancashire in the early sixties he was really fed up. If the ball hit the pad he would mutter 'bloody footballers' over and over again. Very sad really.

I would like to have met him in his prime because I wonder if I would have had to employ the same tactics to frustrate him. Perhaps so, though I like to think not. I

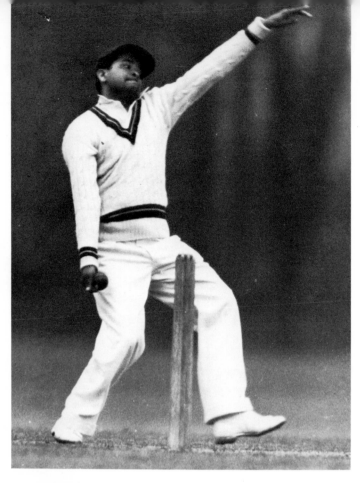

Sonny Ramadhin – a
magnificent bowler finally
frustrated and beaten by the
'bloody footballers'.

Alf Valentine, overshadowed
by his partner but still a
magnificent foil who spun the
ball a great deal.

always play at the ball and try to adjust if it turns; pad-play is not my way. Still, I wonder how my technique would have stood up against a man who was notoriously difficult to read.

An unusual type of bowler I would like to have tried my luck against was Bob Appleyard, who bowled a very quick off-cutter with a distinctive high action and was fearfully difficult to get away. Sometimes he bowled on wet pitches in Yorkshire to a 7-2 field and I'm not sure where on earth batsmen were supposed to hit him in those circumstances.

Appleyard had tremendous stamina as a bowler, in fact once he went on to bowl Norman Yardley had the devil's own job to persuade him to have a rest. And he was a first-class seam bowler who could open the bowling for Yorkshire and nip in a well-disguised seamer when he was supposed to be bowling his cutters. Hutton fielding at slip said he could not pick out Appleyard's disguised seamer which is a compliment indeed, coming from one of the finest batsmen in the game. No wonder Appleyard took 200 wickets in his first season.

Australians remember him as a very important part of England's bowling strategy. After Tyson and Statham they hoped to pick up runs from the change bowlers but Appleyard was so accurate they couldn't afford to take any liberties. They always tell me what a fine bowler he was and it is clear he must have been a very formidable bowler on damp surfaces. Had his career not been cut short by illness he would surely have had a distinguished Test record.

Bradman rated Bill O'Reilly as the greatest bowler he ever played with or against, so I would like to have faced him myself. The interesting thing was that Bradman based his assessment partly on O'Reilly's striking rate – wickets per over as opposed to wickets per run. He must have been a fine bowler to rate such praise from the Great Man himself.

Yorkshire's Maurice Leyland always reckoned he had O'Reilly where he wanted him and the story goes that one day he dared O'Reilly to 'throw him one up' so insistently that the bowler finally lost patience and did just that. Leyland promptly clattered it for four.

I met O'Reilly in 1965 on my first tour of Australia and the first thing he asked was how Maurice was getting on. He also confirmed that the story was true: 'He goaded me and goaded me until out of sheer frustration I tossed him one up and he belted it. That's it, I said, you're not getting another.'

Alan Davidson and Richie Benaud are two more bowlers I would like to have crossed swords with, chiefly because they were both superb exponents of arts which are not seen often enough in the game these days – Davidson the left-arm seamer and Benaud the orthodox leg-spinner.

There have been very few leg-spinners who have made an impact on world cricket in recent years; one or two have flitted in and out without laying claim to a really distinguished career but Benaud took 248 wickets for Australia – more than any other of his countrymen – and still retired at a relatively early age.

Benaud could well be the last of the really great leg-spinners. Intikhab runs him

Unusual and effective –
Yorkshire's Bob Appleyard.
Norman Yardley used to have
the devil's own job persuading
him to take a rest.

Bill O'Reilly, the bowler
Bradman rated the best he
ever played with or against.

Alan Davidson – a tough
apprenticeship in the
shadow of Miller and
Lindwall helped him
develop into the finest left–
arm seamer in the world.

Richie Benaud – the last
of the really great
leg-spinners?

closest in modern times and has done a fine job with Surrey but his record cannot compare with Benaud's at Test level. I batted against Benaud some ten years ago and it was obvious even then that he was a class bowler, a very talented player. Tough and competitive, too, a typical Aussie.

Left-arm seamers attract quite a lot of attention, if only because they usually give most of us right-hand batsman a fair bit of trouble, but there are precious few around these days. Davidson is accepted as being the best ever, challenged only by Sobers for a few years at his prime.

Ken Barrington says Davidson could be really quick when he wished and swung the ball prodigiously. As the ball got older he cut down his pace and bowled tightly: very difficult to score against. Davidson himself admits that a tough apprenticeship in the shadow of Lindwall and Miller helped him a great deal – he rarely got the new ball and usually had to bowl uphill into the wind. He probably moaned about it a bit at the time but he reckons now that it made him a more resilient character and a more complete bowler.

It has become fashionable in Australia to talk about Gary Gilmour as a new Davidson but that is jumping the gun a bit. Davidson took 186 wickets in 44 Test-Matches and Gilmour has quite a bit of ground to make up before he can challenge that.

5

Flair play

No game in the world loves its individuals more than cricket, perhaps because cricket is basically an individual's sport disguised as a team game. There is the reliance of each player on the next, a mutual delight in success or disappointment at failure but responsibility in cricket falls heavily on the individual.

A batsman facing a crisis may have ten thousand supporters and still be the loneliest man in the world, a bowler at the moment of delivery plays in expectant isolation, the man who drops a catch or misfields cannot escape the feeling that every eye on the ground is fixed, often critically, on him alone.

It is the tacit acceptance of their individuality which makes cricketers into characters, even into heroes. The game is rich in folklore woven around individuals, the media are always anxious to explore and develop 'personalities' and if that is an overdeveloped trend these days it is certainly nothing new.

Television and the 'news angle' reporting of cricket by much of the Press threatens to invest players with a sudden star quality beyond their ability and character. A dull day's play can transform a comparatively ordinary performer into an overnight sensation, quickly forgotten. But the field is still rich in genuine personalities, men with proven ability and charisma, the sort of men who Cardus might have 'made up' with fascinating skill. The stuff that legends are made of.

Clive Lloyd at the crease is unlikely-looking hero material. A tall, loose-limbed man with drooping shoulders, features hidden behind dark glasses and beneath a tired sun hat. But Lloyd is power personified, a batsman who can intimidate bowlers with the sheer brutality of his hitting ability.

Lloyd has no great pretensions to batting technique as such. He has a fine eye, superb timing and immense physical strength, the epitome of the weekend slogger except that he hits too straight and too fluently. The slogger hits and hopes, Lloyd bludgeons just as unmercifully but with extraordinary assurance. A heavy bat, a full swing which might have come off a golf range, formidable driving power off the front or back foot. An awe-inspiring sight.

Yorkshire played an early-season Cup tie at Old Trafford in 1975 and Lloyd was facing our off-spinner Geoff Cope. We put mid-off and mid-on well back for the mishit; we know Lloyd doesn't bother with too many singles. Eventually he went

Power personified – Clive Lloyd has no great pretensions to batting technique as such but with his strength and timing, who needs it?

Viv Richards, fired by a determination to dominate the bowler, even when the bowler is Dennis Lillee.

down the pitch and drove Cope fearfully hard – but from where I was standing at mid-wicket he didn't seem to middle it properly. 'Got him,' I thought.

The ball cleared Cope on the up, climbed over our outfielders, whistled over the seats at long-on and disappeared over the sight screen and out of the ground.

John Hampshire came to me between overs with a distinctly pained look on his face. 'I didn't think he'd got hold of that,' he said. 'I'm bloody sure he hit it with the splice,' I replied. 'And look where it's gone. ...'

Lloyd's strength is his strength. He knows it, plays to it quite naturally and I don't think he would have much success if he tried to play any other way. If you do get him in some sort of trouble he simply belts his way out of it as though he takes pleasure in thumping the ball out of shape. I am often asked what I like most about Clive Lloyd and there's no doubt in my mind: his back – and the sooner the better! Too formidable an opponent by half.

When Viv Richards arrived in Somerset six years ago I asked Brian Close what kind of player he was. 'A right-handed Clive Lloyd,' said Closey. I knew we were in for trouble.

Richards is a supremely instinctive batsman whose great strength is an overwhelming desire to dominate the bowler. He revels in a feeling of authority, even to a jaunty, assured swagger to the crease which smacks of arrogance. Richards the man is a quiet, easy-going, friendly sort of person; Richards the batsman is physically powerful, skilful, controlled and quite single-minded. He sets out to dominate and you are left in no doubt about it.

Hooking is his passion – and the more violent the stroke the better he likes it. Not a shot to help the ball on its way but a totally aggressive, explosive attack, a challenge he can rarely resist. When Andy Roberts used to bowl to him it was like a bout between knuckle fighters; Roberts had to bounce him and Richards just had to take him on. A challenge match with no holds barred.

He is surprisingly light on his feet for a big man, quick into position and expert at judging the length of a delivery. He will hit through extra-cover and mid-off but his favourite shots are punched through the leg-side – a legacy of his upbringing in West Indies where the pitches are true, the ball comes on without seaming about and he can align himself confidently to whip shots through the on-side.

A measure of the power in his frame is the fact that he uses a light bat – around 2 lb 7 oz – employs a much shorter backswing than many and can still hit the ball prodigiously hard. Clive Lloyd likes to knock hell out of the ball, Richards prefers a violent sort of caress; the result is often much the same.

If batting is a compulsion to men like Lloyd and Richards it is a philosophy to Majid Khan, one of the most studiously graceful and effortless players in the world. A wonderfully loose-wristed batsman who fashions his strokes with ease and charm, the sort of man who can battle through a difficult situation and still appear utterly composed, even slightly bored.

Majid reminds me of Colin Cowdrey at his best and when I read about the great Ranji and Duleep I often fancy that they must have had his qualities; there is something intangibly Eastern about his approach to the game.

Even when he hooks, normally an aggressive assertion that the bowler cannot have things his own way, Majid tends to cuff the ball rather than attack it. He glides it on its way as if to suggest that the very act of bowling a bouncer to him was an affront. Very calm, quite unruffled.

In early 1977 Pakistan toured Australia and Majid's distinctive bush hat created quite a stir in the Australian camp. Dennis Lillee vowed he would knock it off before the end of the series and tried for two Tests as only Lillee can while Majid breezed along with infuriating aplomb. Needing 31 to win in the Third Test at Sydney, Pakistan lost Sadiq and Zaheer to Lillee before Majid hooked him a couple of times and guided them gently to an eight-wicket win. Then he sought Lillee out and made him a present of ... his hat.

A few seasons ago with Glamorgan Majid was having a desperately thin time, hardly able to piece an innings together. After yet another cheap dismissal he found the groundsman, borrowed a saw and studiously sawed up his bat in the middle of a startled dressing-room – which proves I suppose that even he has his breaking point. Watching him bat you would never believe it.

Majid is a private sort of person, confident of his ability but reluctant to seek publicity, a player with immense dignity. I would never imagine myself having a cross word with him as an opening partner ... and that says a great deal for the man in the heat and tension of professional cricket.

England has seen little of Graeme Pollock, the big, slow-moving South African who times the ball so sweetly and hits so powerfully – and that is due largely to his endearing honesty. Pollock has had plenty of offers from English Counties but he admits that the idea of a long, arduous season on unfamiliar pitches does not really appeal; he stays at home when he might have accepted a lucrative contract and done just enough to safeguard his reputation. Others have.

Pollock remains the charismatic figure in South African cricket, a man who can capture attention simply by his presence on the ground. Deceptively fluent in his runmaking, he can build major innings with a speed which belies the culture and control of his batsmanship, rarely appearing to force the pace.

He hits superbly on the up, loves to drive the ball off back or front foot – a facility encouraged by the true pitches in South Africa – and can flash the ball through the off-side with amazing ferocity. Sir Don Bradman saw him demoralize Australia with a double century early in the sixties and was captivated by a batsman who played 'rather like a latter-day Frank Woolley'.

The natural line of a right-hand bowler tends to go across a left-hand batsman and Pollock drives through the covers and round to point with superb strength and timing. If the bowler attacks leg stump to keep him quiet, he makes room and still hits through the off; so the bowler is committed to bowling wide of the leg stump and then Pollock has a free hit behind square or over mid-wicket. It is a familiar enough pattern but few bowlers have found a way of avoiding the trap.

He has the good pitch player's limitations when the ball seams or turns, chiefly

LEFT Majid Khan . . . a distinctive line in sunhats and a useful performer with a crosscut saw when things go wrong . . .
RIGHT Hitting on the up – a typically fluent shot from South Africa's Graeme Pollock.

LEFT Barry Richards – his biggest flaw is a lack of down-to-earth professionalism
RIGHT Down to business – Greg Chappell, correct and stylish but alert and aggressive.

because he has had relatively little experience on any except true surfaces. But there is no doubting his class; an hour spent watching Pollock is an exhilarating experience.

Barry Richards can be a classically impressive player and an endlessly frustrating one. His basic game is suited to good pitches but he has learned enough in a decade of English County cricket to play reasonably well on poorer surfaces which spin and seam; at his best he looks first rate – straight, fluent, a fine driver of the ball.

Richards does not take kindly to being tied down and invariably tries to improvise, using his feet to disconcert the spinners, happy to sweep. It often works, but it sometimes costs him his wicket unnecessarily.

His biggest weakness is not a technical flaw but a lack of down-to-earth professionalism. He likes to command the stage, to be the centre of attention, and he claimed he could not play well as often as he was expected to in County cricket. He insisted he needed the stimulus of a big occasion, and perhaps he retired from County cricket because he felt it was not big enough for him.

Well, every professional cricketer likes the big occasion, large crowds, atmosphere, but most also realize that they owe it to their team, their County club and their spectators to try to raise their game in every match, difficult though that may be. I might try like hell and get twenty runs, Richards may score as many without effort – no difference in the end result but at least I could not be accused of not trying my hardest.

I would have liked to bat with Richards because I think we could have learned something from each other. Our styles are different, our approach to the game is different and perhaps something of mutual benefit might have rubbed off. Perhaps he might have acquired a bit more mental toughness. Richards on a good day is a fine player to watch but from a man of his talent there should be more good days.

Greg Chappell treats batting like a business. He walks to the wicket with the brisk, bustling air of a man looking forward to clocking in for a full day's work, perhaps an hour or two of overtime, and he is always difficult to dislodge once he has got on to his favourite foot.

England was well aware of his preference for playing off the front foot during the Test series in 1977 and our bowlers made a conscious effort to force him back but that is easier said than done. Once there, he drives fluently between extra-cover and mid-off and turns the ball powerfully into the mid-on, mid-wicket area. He has also developed a shot which is characteristically his own, whipping the ball which lifts into his body from just short of a length away through mid-wicket with exceptional severity.

Chappell is a class batsman and looks every inch the part. Unfussy, well-balanced, aggressive enough to thump the medium-pacer over mid-on but fundamentally very correct and stylish.

His responsibilities in England in the 1977 series were especially formidable because he was clearly Australia's most accomplished player, the man every bowler was looking to dismiss cheaply. I told him months before the tour started that it would be the hardest he had ever undertaken and events bore that out. Chappell knew more was expected of him than any other player in the team, he demanded more from himself and that put an unavoidable extra burden on his shoulders. When he most needed to relax he was at his most tense. Even so, he looked head and shoulders above any other Australian batsman.

Gloucestershire's Zaheer Abbas – 'Z Man' to the county players – is an exceptionally talented batsman, a marvellous player off the back foot. He likes to hook though he isn't particularly good at it and once he has established himself no bowler dares take liberties outside the off stump. Given any room there, Zaheer loves to belt the ball through the covers.

His determination to stay back whenever possible makes Zaheer a little vulnerable early in an innings but he has adjusted remarkably well to the varying conditions of County cricket and his career record shows he has the concentration and temperament to build a big innings. He prefers a good slow pitch to a good quick one and he is an adroit player of spin. With that high flowing backlift he is a fluent and graceful player – a free and easy scorer of runs to the delight of his many admirers.

Spin bowling is the most deceitful, devious art in cricket, the most inscrutable and in many ways the most difficult of skills for the spectator to appreciate. Like a schoolboy's Shakespeare, full of tricky shades and meanings, it takes some learning. But there are few real cricket lovers who do not regard top-class spin bowling as a pleasure to be prized above all others in the game and there is no better exponent of his craft than India's Bishen Bedi.

Bedi prancing in to bowl in a brightly-coloured patka captures everything creative and beautiful in the spinners' game. Suppleness, ease of movement, grace, balance, a perfect high action, the ball delivered with a flowing freedom which is perfectly controlled. The batsman becomes momentarily superfluous; Bedi is an entertainment in himself.

Having such a superb action, Bedi can vary his deliveries with a minimum of adjustment. He has so much control at the point of delivery that if a batsman anticipates his intentions and tries to improvise Bedi can alter length, line or both without any perceptible change in his rhythm. He stays one step ahead. Through the air the ball loops high but dips very quickly so that few batsmen are able to drive him on the ground through the covers, which is where a left-arm bowler should be hit most easily. Batting against him is often a harrowing mixture of panic and desperation.

The first move is confident enough until a batsman finds he has not quite got to the pitch of the ball. Then he adjusts hurriedly and blocks, tries to slog over the top, sweeps if the ball pitches leg and middle and he thinks he can get away with it or tries to lap off the stumps as a desperate measure. If Bedi goes for runs it is usually because someone has slogged him and got away with it.

Sadly I think he has suffered from playing too much County cricket. Players got used to him over the years, which usually meant they were more wary than ever; Bedi seemed to become jaded and rather frustrated at times. He is a charming and

Zaheer Abbas likes to hook although he isn't particularly adept at it. A marvellous player off the back foot.

An entertainment in himself: Bishen Bedi captures everything creative and beautiful in the spinners' game.

courteous opponent but he knows he could have done with more striking performances in County cricket, more facts and figures and he sometimes tried too many variations as though he was a little bored and dispirited. Batsmen were generally negative out of respect for his ability and that is a frustrating price to pay for so much expertise.

Derek Underwood has the face of a choirboy, the demeanour of a civil servant and the ruthlessness of a rat catcher. Watching him bowl is watching the complete professional at work. I never cease to marvel at the concentration, stamina and patience of the man.

Underwood is a mean pressure bowler who gives absolutely nothing away and expects nothing in return. If he bowls a bad delivery – which is rare enough – he expects an alert batsman to hit it for four. But he resents a sneaky single and he bowls every delivery as though he expects it to go just where he wants it to go and do exactly what he wants it to do. Every delivery is bowled with such meticulous care that he is disappointed if he doesn't take a wicket every time.

His style is unique – and that is a much misused word – in world cricket. Quicker than the stock left-arm spinner, a flatter trajectory and a form of leg cutter rather than pure spin, he is amazingly accurate and he varies his overs with subtleties which are fiendishly difficult for a batsman to read. On a wet pitch he will bowl out any side in the world.

If I had to compare him with another bowler I think Underwood is a sort of left-handed Bob Appleyard. He bowled faster than the usual spinner, had immense control and bowled a sort of cutter. But really Underwood is in a category and a class of his own.

In a wry way I enjoy a confrontation with him on a damp pitch. He puts a batsman's skill to the supreme test and to succeed for an hour against him is a real achievement. The ball will turn, bounce, and lift most alarmingly and the only batsman likely to get runs against him in those circumstances is the left-hander who can hit with the spin who may get away with it once or twice before he is winkled out.

When he was first chosen for England there were many who advised him to bowl slower, to give the ball more air and look for more variation in his overs. He listened to them, naturally enough because he wanted to improve, but they were thinking in terms of a conventional left-arm spinner – and his unorthodoxy is Underwood's greatest strength.

He pins batsmen down until panic sets in, squeezes them in a vice until they have no patience left and attempt something desperate simply to snatch a run. Then they commit suicide.

I remember a story about Wilfred Rhodes, the greatest Yorkshireman of them all, who tied down a batsman of Victor Trumper's authority for over after over with his own brand of selfish left-arm spin. Trumper finally leaned wearily on his bat and said, 'Please, Wilfred, please give me some peace.' Many a batsman has muttered that to Underwood, the modern master.

The face of a choirboy, the demeanour of a civil servant, the ruthlessness of a rat-catcher – Derek Underwood the complete professional.

Craftsmanship – and in an all-too-rare craft at that – is the hallmark of Intikhab Alam, a player whose impact on the English County cricket scene with Surrey has been incalculable. Intikhab is still the world's leading exponent of wrist-spin at the age of 38, an art which flourishes in Pakistan and to a lesser extent in Australia but which has become almost extinct in County cricket. The game in England would have lacked a wonderfully intriguing craft without him.

Intikhab has superb control and bowls remarkably few loose deliveries for a leg-spinner. If he does take punishment he reacts phlegmatically, keeps cool and concentrates on the next delivery – a mental toughness which has enabled him to bowl all over the world with success and perform in limited-overs cricket with distinction. Even in a one-day match batsmen are reluctant to chance their arm, which says a great deal for the mystery of the man.

He bowls flatter in limited-over matches but he can still produce his variations – the googly and top-spinner. In a three-day game he throws the ball up, chiefly to encourage the batsmen to attack him and make mistakes. He has a very good quick flipper which he sometimes runs into the batsman for variety, a tricky top-spinner, occasional googly and leg-spin with endless variations of pace and flight. A kaleidoscope of possibilities.

It has become fashionable to bemoan the absence of genuinely fast bowlers in County cricket and with some justification but the game has suffered from a lack of wrist-spinners far longer and in some ways more seriously. Intikhab has kept his trade alive in England; it is a great pity there are not many more to follow in his footsteps. I feel sad that he is coming to the end of his career and with Surrey already having two other overseas players he is gradually being phased out of the game.

One incident on a sunny afternoon in Sydney in 1971 summed up the quality of a wicket-keeper who, for me, has already achieved the ultimate in top-class cricket.

It was the Fifth Test, Ray Illingworth was bowling and Greg Chappell was finally drawn on to a delivery which turned between bat and pad and left him momentarily stranded. Alan Knott missed the stumping – and ten England team-mates were so stunned that nobody knew what to say. There was a long embarrassed silence.

That was Knott's first mistake in four and a half months on tour. He had taken good catches, brilliant catches, and never missed a stumping. The thought that he might actually let that standard slip had never occurred to anyone – and the standard was frighteningly high.

Knott has achieved so much as a wicket-keeper-batsman that we tend to expect the impossible. It is a compliment and a responsibility which he can carry only because he asks perfection from himself – perfection in his equipment, in his approach to the match, in his preparation for the next delivery.

Knott behind the wicket is endless movement. Stretching, twisting, bending, taking an imaginary catch on this side, then the other. It is amusing, even irritating, but it is based on a belief that every exercise might just help him to take the catch which he feels certain will arrive with the next ball. He is totally absorbed in the game, quite single-minded. If it could be proved that standing on his head would

LEFT Intikhab Alam – wily and mentally tough, keeping alive a threatened trade.
RIGHT Alan Knott strikes again. If it could be proved that standing on his head would make him a better wicket-keeper, Knott would do it.

A risky business, taking a run into the area patrolled by Derek Randall. He has a gift which I hope he never loses, the ability to clown and yet concentrate.

make him a better wicket-keeper, Knott would happily do it.

He spends hours checking over his equipment, adjusting and kneading it until it is perfectly comfortable, hour after hour smacking a ball into the palm of his glove until it is a leather replica of his hand. No man would devote years of his life to that kind of meticulous preparation simply through exhibitionism; he is a perfectionist with impossibly high standards and he deserves every bit of the success which that has brought.

His supreme professionalism also shows in the way he has developed his batting over the years. He was basically a defensive player, able to cut and work the ball on the leg-side, nothing special. But he worked at it, developed confidence and a wider range of shots and now loves to take on the quicker bowlers or go down the pitch to spinners.

Knott has saved England so many times when their situation was close to desperation that his resilience became legendary. Heroics were expected from him and whether he was battling out of a tight situation or helping to put the opposition under pressure, Knott was an inspiration. He was the best wicket-keeper I have ever seen or am likely to see and he deserves to be remembered as one of the all-time great players. I can think of no higher tribute than that.

You can't write about the best players in the game without including Derek Randall for his fielding alone. His strength is his ability to anticipate where the batsman intends to seek a single. He challenges you to match your pace against his reactions and he is amazingly quick off the mark.

His exuberance on the field makes him especially dangerous because it is difficult to pinpoint his position. I always study field placings and try to memorize them before I face a delivery but with Randall there is never any certainty that he will be where you expect him. He stands deep but as the bowler runs in he walks forward, skips, jogs a pace or two ... and by the time you play a stroke he is fifteen yards closer than you remember and closing fast. Very disconcerting.

Randall saves runs on his reputation because batsmen are increasingly unwilling to take him on and he likes to play on that. He will challenge a batsman to run, amble towards the ball smiling and beckoning him to risk it. Yet his concentration never wavers. Even when he is playing to the crowd – flicking the ball to hand with his heel, dropping his cap and flicking it on to his head – he is always aware of the batsman's position, the possibilities of the situation. He can clown and yet concentrate, even amid the pressure of a Test Match, and that is a gift which I hope he never loses.

Rick McCosker underestimated him briefly at Headingley in 1977 and paid a heavy price. McCosker had backed up only a couple of paces at the non-striker's end when he was sent back; he had not ventured far and there was no reason to suppose he was in any real danger. But Randall had spotted him edging forward a couple of deliveries earlier and was ready to pounce with incredible speed. Poor McCosker was brilliantly run out and if it is any consolation, there will be plenty of others.

Tony Greig is assured of some sort of place in cricket history – fame or notoriety, depending on your view of the Packer Affair and its impact on the game worldwide.

He is a successful businessman in Australia now, head of an insurance firm and his immediate involvement in cricket seems limited to commenting on television for Packer's Channel Nine. On the face of it, it looks as if his playing days are over but with a man like him there is no knowing what his latest adventure might be. He is desperately difficult to categorize in cricket but his worst enemy would not deny that Greig has plenty of flair. He is basically a show-off, an incorrigible extrovert who decided early in his career that anything was better than being ignored. He has worked on his image every bit as hard as he has worked on his cricket.

He had a head start – a head and shoulders start really since at 6 ft 7½ ins it was never exactly difficult to spot him on the field. And Greig projected himself astutely, searching out the limelight whenever possible, manufacturing excitement on the field to the delight of some and the annoyance of the older school.

Whatever one's attitude towards Greig's antics or his involvement with Kerry Packer his performances at Test level indicate that he is a very fine player. He competes hard, he is determined and he loves success, needs it to feed his ego. When Greig has done well he loves people to say so to his face; many players are happy to escape to a quiet meal or a couple of hours in front of the TV. Greig likes to go out on the town, to be seen and recognized. Success is like a drug.

It has always been difficult to categorize him in the England team and his critics claim with some justification that he was neither a good enough batsman nor a good enough bowler with batting as his second string to command a place. But his Test record says he is a very effective all-rounder – and facts and figures are the yardstick of any professional cricketer's career.

His bowling has never been quite up to third seamer standard in a good England team but that has not prevented him from taking 129 Test wickets and in a style which may amuse or infuriate but which is certainly all his own. Inevitably he play-acts.

A long stare calculated to annoy or upset the batsman, a few strong words muttered as he passes at the end of an over, arms raised skywards in exasperation if a batsman plays and misses or pads up ... leave a delivery and Greig will insist it missed the off stump by a hairbreadth, survive a good delivery and he is likely to bend double as if no mortal deserved to get away with that. It is contrived, histrionic, and Greig makes no secret of its purpose: a deliberate policy to project himself and make the public aware of his presence. Like it or loathe it, there is no accident about it, and Greig rarely went unnoticed during his career in English cricket.

Greig's bowling style takes him close in to the stumps at delivery and he bowls mainly out-swing varied with in-seamers. He discovered during the 1974 tour of West Indies that his seamers were not up to scratch on their pitches and he was shrewd enough to persuade himself and others that he could bowl off-cutters. They paid off in the Fifth Test but his success was deceptive; his off-cutters have very little to recommend them.

As a batsman, Greig has prospered because he plays to his strengths – basically,

Anything is better than being ignored to the incorrigible extrovert Tony Greig.
He has worked on his image every bit as hard as he has worked on his game – but his
performances insist he is a very fine player.

his enormous height and reach. He plays and misses often, lacking the technique of a class batsman but his reach gives him a fundamental advantage which he uses effectively.

The fashion for short-pitched bowling which worried cricket authorities troubled Greig less than most because his height allowed him to get over the ball and play deliveries off his chest which would have threatened the throat of most batsmen. He is aggressive by nature and a powerful driver on the up, making the most of his long stride.

For a big man Greig is an exceptionally sure second slip – the best tall slip fielder I have ever seen. He gets down very quickly, has an enormous reach and a remarkably safe pair of hands.

Few players have channelled strength, speed and elemental power into their bowling more successfully or dramatically than Mike Procter. The most bone-shaking action among quick bowlers is also one of the most effective – at his best he ranks with the most formidable of fast men.

Procter's long run is all effort and passion. He does not glide in as many do, he thunders in with his chest heaving, the ground shaking beneath his feet. At the moment of delivery he is going so fast that he cannot pivot or bring himself sideways on, he simply launches his body, his arm and the ball in one explosion. It is a fearsome sight.

A popular misconception is that he delivers the ball off the wrong foot. In fact he catapults himself forward just before his left foot reaches the ground so that he does not pivot himself as most bowlers do. Either way it is pretty disconcerting for the batsman, especially the one facing him for the first time. The ball comes on before you expect it and it takes time to work him out.

Batsmen tend to use their pads against him a lot because he bowls wide of the crease, and that, plus his booming in-swing, makes it desperately difficult to get an lbw decision from over the wicket. From round the wicket he is a very different proposition; bowling accurately at a very demanding pace and pitching the ball just outside off stump so that his swing makes it perfectly possible to win lbw decisions. I watched from the other end when he took a hat-trick against Yorkshire at Cheltenham last year and there was not the slightest doubt about any of the decisions.

'Procky' swings the ball prodigiously, so much so that although he bowls round the wicket more often than any fast bowler I know. He is like an off-spinner bowling round the wicket on a turning pitch. Occasionally he rolls his fingers over the seam to push through a straight one and that, after several deliveries which have cut in sharply, is as effective as an out-swinger.

Fast bowlers have always enjoyed a special place in cricket and its folklore. As men they command an especially healthy respect off the field, as though even the spectators suspect they might suddenly revert to type and break a head or two. As players they can hold a match spellbound, and dominate the spectacle of an afternoon.

The fastest bowler in the world – Michael Holding has a splendidly clean, uncluttered style, a sprinter's action and the sort of speed which destroys.

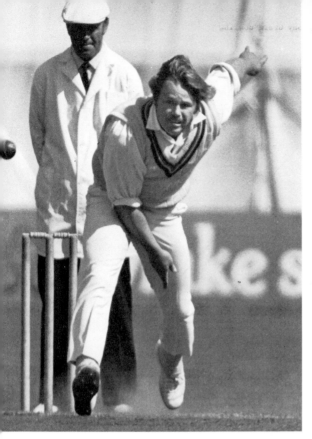

LEFT Few bowlers generate as much strength, speed and power as Mike Procter.
RIGHT Andy Roberts – a clever, scheming bowler who'd be dangerous at half his pace.

LEFT The publicity men did a good job on Jeff Thomson, the renegade who was sure to knock hell out of the Poms. His performances can speak for themselves.
RIGHT Endless variety at 90mph – Dennis Lillee is a very formidable proposition.

Players, if they are honest enough to admit it, share some of the common dread of the really quick bowler. The prospect of meeting a really formidable fast man tranquillizes the liveliest dressing-room and creates an atmosphere of tension and apprehension; the earliest overs are watched with special interest by those waiting to go in. There is a distinct lack of volunteers for nightwatchman.

Part of the fast bowler's fascination must lie in the fact that his is a totally hostile profession. The knowledge that somebody might get hurt is half alarming, half appealing; nobody wants it to happen but nobody wants to miss it if it does. Batsmen blot the possibility of injury from their minds but they can never escape the atmosphere which fast bowlers create.

West Indies discovered an especially formidable trio in 1976, including a young man whom I first came across six years ago on Mike Denness' tour. He was tall and gangling then, quite thin, no more than medium-fast and he played for Jamaica against the touring team. Now Michael Holding is accepted by most batsmen as the fastest bowler in the world; an athlete with a devastating turn of speed.

Some fast bowlers radiate menace. Holding's approach to the wicket is smooth and languid, the action of a sprinter with elbows tucked into his sides, head erect. But the speed of his delivery is phenomenal. Like many really fast bowlers in their heyday he does not 'do' much with the ball off the pitch; at his pace he does not have to. A marvellously clean, uncluttered style, speed and a devastating yorker wreaked havoc with England four years ago.

Andy Roberts may lack some of Holding's speed – which at their pace is purely relative – but he is an intelligent thinking bowler who varies his overs disconcertingly and adjusts his plan of attack to suit different surfaces.

Roberts is almost two men. Very shy and reserved off the field, happier coaching youngsters or playing records in his room than meeting people. Very dark-browed and menacing, he is unsmiling and preoccupied with the job in hand. He has a shortish run for a bowler of his speed but he generates tremendous action in relatively few strides and delivers the ball with a sideways lean which flattens its trajectory; the ball skims on to the bat at his normal pace. He has an excellent slower ball, a very testing bouncer and a wicked yorker. A clever, scheming bowler who would be dangerous at half his pace.

Somebody did a good job on Jeff Thomson when he burst to prominence in the Ashes series five years ago. He was projected as the renegade, the hard-living, hard-swearing fast bowler who was going to knock hell out of the Poms and love every minute of it. What did Thomson like most in life? Birds, lots of them. And after that? The sight of Pom blood. It was an appealing combination for the Australian public who like nothing more than to see the English being beaten out of sight. An outrageous image but well projected and if Thomson did not actually say many of the things attributed to him he was in no hurry to deny them.

By the time he got round to denying many of the more lurid stories and quotes attributed to him it was too late. He had a vivid image on which the public could feed its imagination; and his exploits on the field were quite amazing.

Yet Thomson the Test player is a restrained, even placid, man. He may unleash a few colourful Aussie remarks if he has bowled a bad delivery or the batsman has played a particularly good shot, but he is not one for histrionics. His performance can speak for him – and eloquently at that.

Thomson is beautifully built for a fast bowler. Average height, very strong in the shoulders and back, legs powerful without being too thick. His run up is not too long but not a pace is wasted and his unusual slinging action delivers the ball at real speed. More than that, it generates exceptional bounce, even from full-length deliveries, which are extremely difficult to counter.

Unusually, Thomson prefers the ball when it is a few overs old because he has difficulty in controlling a new ball. Some of his most erratic spells are bowled when the ball is new and will swing unpredictably. He likes hard surfaces to make the most of his bounce, swings the ball out and can seam it either way off the pitch. His partnership with Dennis Lillee has already won a place in the history of the game.

Lillee must surely be remembered as one of the greatest fast bowlers the game has ever seen. That superb action alone – powerful and rhythmic, beautifully balanced and classically side-on at delivery – is worth a place in any hall of fame. He reminds me forcibly of Fred Trueman and I can think of no bigger compliment than that.

Like Fred, Lillee is a thinking bowler who uses his speed to the utmost effect but does not rely wholly on pace for his success. Facing him demands every ounce of a batsman's concentration and skill because there is always so much going on.

Lillee is always trying to deceive. He varies his pace, length, position and angle of delivery so that two consecutive deliveries are rarely the same. Even his bouncer is a teaser; one will come through at a comparatively gentle pace so you think you can hook, the next is a yard and a half quicker and if you are trapped hooking the chances are they will have to stretcher you out of harm's way. Endless variety bowled at around 90 mph: a very formidable proposition.

As his reputation increased over the years Lillee became increasingly conscious of his image. He plays to the gallery more than ever these days – a typical fast bowler's repertoire full of angry gestures, scowls and rich oaths. Again like Fred, he loves to involve the crowd in his assault on the batsmen and the crowd love to see him do it.

Batsmen, not unnaturally, are less impressed. It is never easy to concentrate while Lillee is having an attack of the verbals but I have found that if he is seen to be ignored he soon tires of the theatricals and gets back to business.

Umpires are not usually associated with the entertainment value of cricket, in fact there is a strong tradition which insists they should be seen and not heard. Dickie Bird is quite impossible to ignore.

I used to play in the Yorkshire League with Dickie at Barnsley and even then he was renowned for the nervous twitching gestures which delight or infuriate so many people today. Sometimes he was so nervous before going in to bat I had to put his gloves on for him.

When he took up umpiring many people were afraid he would not stand the

Dickie Bird is acknowledged as the world's top umpire, even if his mannerisms often infuriate those who know him least. Dickie hasn't changed in twenty years and those who think he is playing for the cameras simply don't know the man.

pressure but he has bridged the gap with amazing success. He is definitely England's top umpire now – and that is not just my opinion. It is borne out by his marks from County Captain's reports during the season and by the number of Test Matches in which he has been asked to stand.

His mannerisms are famous – or notorious. Stooping over the wickets like a vulture, short coat tucked up beneath his arms, peering from beneath a penguin cap with arms flicking, wrists twirling. A bundle of nervous energy.

But the players respect him because they know he is always in charge, concentrating on every delivery. He will have a chat with players he knows and can throw back a cutting reply with the best of them if he is challenged while remaining firm and authoritative, friendly but not familiar.

He is very positive, always determined to get on with the game as quickly as possible, ready to gallop to the pavilion to sort matters out if necessary – and that cannot be bad from the spectators' point of view. Yet he is never hasty when it comes to making a decision; he will give himself a second or two to collect his thoughts and weigh the pros and cons. Players appreciate that approach more than an umpire, right or wrong, who fires off an instant decision.

Off the field he is great company, a wonderful teller of tales punctuated with all the old familiar gestures. That is the point about Dickie – he is entirely natural. His gestures come as readily to him now as they did twenty years ago when I first knew him and he was a long, long way from being a Test umpire.

Those who suggest it is affectation do not know the man. If you asked Dickie Bird to cut out all his mannerisms, to slow down and stop getting into the action quite so often he really would not know what you were talking about.

Nottinghamshire's Clive Rice has benefited enormously from his experiences in English County cricket; in fact, there is little doubt that the last three years have been the most important in his career. When I first saw Clive in South Africa he was struggling to make his provincial side; not many years later he is undoubtedly a world class all-rounder.

Anyone who doubts that has only to consider his season with World Series Cricket, when he won over many people who had not seen him play before and might have challenged his claim to be top class. His seasons in the English game have helped Clive to express himself; they have given him a sound standard against which to judge his own ability. He got involved, realized he was better than most of the players around him and set about proving it match after match.

Like most South Africans Clive is deeply and fiercely competitive. Unlike some, he is quiet and undemonstrative; he doesn't go in for a great deal of showmanship or histrionics on the field. He lets his performances do the talking, and his particular brand of heartfelt, silent hostility is the more daunting for it.

He is a difficult bowler to counter because he bowls a deceptive length. His deliveries are always slightly fuller than you expect so that if a batsman plays back – the natural tendency against quick bowling – he often finds himself in trouble with the ball skimming through at a very respectable pace.

Clive generates his pace from a long swing of the arm and full use of the body on the follow-through. He literally throws his whole body after the ball and follows a long way down the pitch, which means that the ball hits the ground hard and he gets a skimming sort of bounce from a full length; very awkward. His standard delivery swings away and sometimes nips back; bowled with his natural hostility and at his pace it is a handful. Yet for all his menace Clive is not bouncer happy. He probably bowls fewer bouncers than most bowlers of comparable speed.

As a batsman Clive could be held up as a model to aspiring youngsters in one important respect: he is a fine example of the theory that if you pick the bat up straight you will bring it down straight and drive well.

He has an exaggerated sideways-on stance and lifts the bat before the ball is delivered *à la* Tony Greig. The left elbow is bent, cocked ready to put power into his stroke and his weight is usually slightly forward; he is already leaning into the drive. It is as if Clive has worked hard on the belief that a straight, full backlift is the essential part of a good cricket shot and although his style may lack the smoothness of some – it does tend to look a little stage-managed – there is no doubting the basic correctness of his approach; nor its effectiveness. Ask mid-off or mid-on when they are being driven back steadily towards the boundary. ...

He does not look to hook or pull much but he drives so positively and with so much strength that that is not necessarily a disadvantage. He can hit through the ball in a wide arc on either side of the pitch.

Playing against Oxford University at The Parks some years ago I came across a young player who batted impressively and bowled a useful but not exceptional medium pace. While I was batting against him I got the impression that Imran Khan had something to give which he was not quite getting out of himself; he bowled medium-pace without the action or attitude of a genuine medium-pacer. I felt he was a quick bowler who didn't know it.

In 1976 I was in Australia, playing at Waverley, when I was asked to do a TV commentary on Queensland's match against the Pakistan tourists. Pakistan's captain, Mushtaq, was concerned at their lack of success with the ball; they simply were not bowling sides out and he asked me what I thought. I told him that Imran was wasted as a durable medium-pacer. He should bowl really quick for five or six overs and be used in short bursts if necessary.

In the second innings against Queensland Imran bowled really quick; not long afterwards he bowled out the Aussies in the Test Match at Sydney, bowling for enormously long spells with an amazing mixture of speed and stamina. It was as though he had discovered reserves of strength in his body and a new awareness of his own abilities. I don't for a moment take credit for it but it is satisfying to be proved right now that Imran is clearly one of the world's great all-rounders.

There is nothing particularly aesthetic about Imran's bowling action. He bowls wide of the crease and pretty chest-on, a strong man's action rather than a thing of flowing beauty. But he has the genuine strength of a born athlete, a marvellously tough frame which generates real speed and amazing stamina. He is a better bowler

LEFT Clive Rice – a fierce competitor who lets his performances do the talking.
RIGHT Imran Khan – a fast bowler who didn't know it until a Test Match in Sydney.

A familiar round of congratulations for Ian Botham, alias Guy the Gorilla – the most physically frightening player in the England dressing-room. Botham's overwhelming self-confidence intimidates opponents; he will make a formidable England captain.

now that he has perfected his line outside the off stump; a natural in-swing bowler and in those early days in Australia he tended to bowl at the stumps too much which allowed batsmen to play him down the leg-side.

Imran the batsman had made a reputation at Oxford long before he went to Worcestershire and developed his County and International career. He is a natural stroke-maker, a free and uninhibited striker of the ball who is not afraid to use his strength to pull or hook violently, and on top of his natural talents Imran is also a splendid competitor and a great guy. I have always admired him as a man and as a cricketer.

Somerset's Ian Botham is more than a cricketer with a breathtakingly golden future. He is a phenomenon. I have never known a player combine so much physical strength, aggression and ability into one package.

Physically, Ian is massive. Huge, strong shoulders and chest; thick, solid legs and a fast bowler's backside which is always threatening to split his flannels at the seams. It was the Duke of Wellington, I think, who looked at his soldiers and said, 'I don't know what they do to the enemy but, my God, they frighten me'. Ian has that sort of effect in the England dressing-room.

I don't think there is anyone in the England side who is not secretly worried that Ian will decide to be playful and smash a rib or two with a friendly hug. A couple of years ago I nicknamed him 'Guy' after the gorilla which eventually died, much lamented, at London Zoo. The name stuck – but 'Guy' is an intelligent gorilla, let there be no doubt about that.

He often gives the impression that he doesn't think too deeply about what he is doing and there is no doubt that he is quite capable of flying off at a headstrong tangent if things do not go the way he would like. But that is part of his uncomplicated, physical approach to the game and I suspect it is also part of a protective blind, an image which he does not resent just as long as the results are right.

If there is one single secret of Ian's success it must be his enormous self-confidence. I cannot recall his ever doubting that he would take wickets or score runs or probably both. And his confidence is so tangible that it tends to overpower opponents, even if Ian does not always realize the effect he is having. They cannot intimidate him or demoralize him because if he fails with the bat he is quite convinced he will murder them with the ball; if he does not take wickets he simply reminds them that he is a great batsman and they had better watch it. Big-headed? I suppose he might be accused of that were it not for the fact that he invariably puts his performances where his mouth is. Look at the records and try telling yourself that Ian is a myth.

People keep insisting that the bubble will burst, that Ian will lose his magic touch and find it impossible to deal with failure simply because he has enjoyed so much success. I don't think the bubble will burst at all. It may be a smaller bubble on some days but I suspect Ian will always have success simply because he is such a talented player; there is no fluke about his extraordinary impact on the game. Unless he is bedevilled by injuries I can see no reason why Ian should not go on and on and on.

I fancied that he would make a very good England captain one day, though I hoped the responsibility wouldn't be thrust on him too soon. He deserves time to be exuberant and brash, to live and enjoy his game without too many extra pressures. He has been in the happy position of being able to be outrageous and people may judge him on that, concluding he hasn't the depth or maturity to make a good captain. I think they are wrong.

Ian has the enormous advantage of being able to lead from the front; when the chips are down players naturally look to a captain to pull them through by the strength of his performance. They like to feel they can lean on the skipper's ability and he won't let them down. There have been exceptions to this, of course – Mike Brearley was a good captain without being the best player in the England side – but I feel that players generally prefer a captain who can show them as well as tell them how it's done.

There is absolutely no doubt that Ian is in that class. And I know that he will take his responsibilities seriously, although I would have preferred to see him groomed for a couple of years before being given the job. I would have liked him to have sewn his wild oats while he could but now he has it, I want him to succeed.

Botham the bowler has two distinct styles. If conditions are suitable or he is using the new ball, he will cut down his pace to a genuine medium-pace, pitch the ball up to give it a chance to swing and encourage the batsman to drive. A real swing bowler trying to outwit the batsman.

The other Botham is probably more familiar, trying to bowl at a lively pace often rather quicker than he should or can. A bouncer or two and lots of variety because Ian is never happy to see the game simply progress. He wants something to happen and if it looks a bit tame he will do his level best to force a change in the pattern, to upset the batsman's rhythm and balance. Sometimes it looks a bit unthinking – if he is hurling down bouncers and being hooked for his pains – but it is really just the opposite. It is Ian's way of making waves and he is prepared to take a bit of hammer just to breathe vitality back into the contest. He is nobody's fool. His action is good; side-on, full of strength and power with a really big pivot of the body.

As a batsman Ian is always hankering to hit the ball out of sight. It's his natural game and he has found that it pays for him, so why should he change? If he tried to curb himself he would certainly be much less effective.

One big point in his favour is that as a genuine all-rounder he does not need to rely too much on his batting alone. He reckons that if he does not come off with the bat he will bowl a side out instead; and that gives him the confidence to go for his shots in a wholehearted, uninhibited way – a formidable sight.

He lets his shots flow, bats with great freedom and uses his pent-up strength to launch many a bowler into orbit. His best shot is probably that magnificent pick-up on the leg-side. Most batsmen would be happy to play square or just behind square for a couple; Ian launches himself into the stroke and when he connects properly there's not much change out of six.

When I first encountered Wayne Daniel as a young bowler at the Scarborough Festival I suggested to him he would be well advised to concentrate on a more side-on action. Wayne studiously ignored me, continued to bowl with that chest-on, splay-footed action and is sending them down faster than ever these days. So much for good advice ...

Daniel is quick. I rate him among the six fastest bowlers in the world and as such it is perhaps surprising that he does not bowl more short stuff than he does. But he is one of the few really fast bowlers who rarely bowls short of a length; his stock delivery is of a fullish length and that may be due to the fact that he has played most of his mature cricket in English conditions.

He is also a thinking, intelligent bowler who uses English conditions well. Not that there is anything particularly attractive in his action – especially from the receiving end – but he has bags of stamina and always runs in with purpose and aggression. He looks somewhat musclebound but that does not detract from his effectiveness and he bowls a devastating yorker, sliding into the batsman from wide of the crease and fearfully difficult to counter. I was amazed that Wayne was left out of the West Indies squad for the 1979 World Cup and then for their subsequent tour of Australia; it simply shows what a wealth of fast bowling talent they have at their disposal.

One bowler who certainly stands head and shoulders above all others in the West Indies' camp is Joel Garner – a man I have no hesitation in nominating as the most difficult bowler in the world for a batsman to score runs against. There are faster bowlers, because Garner is not among the genuine quicks, but there is nobody quite as awkward as the 'Big Bird'.

Garner is tall – something of an understatement for a man who stands 6 ft 8 ins – bowls with a high arm action and leaps into his delivery stride for good measure. The result is that facing him is like confronting a bowler on stilts; the ball hits the pitch hard and invariably bounces at least twelve inches higher than normal, even off a good length.

It is almost impossible to play forward because the ball is always thumping into the splice or rearing towards the chest. During the World Cup final Joel bowled from the Nursery End at Lord's and by the time he released the ball his arm was way above the sight screen. It's no fun being bowled at from a height of ten or eleven feet!

A unique combination of natural height and a high delivery action means that Joel gets prodigious bounce, especially on hard surfaces, and there are times when you despair of getting a run against him. He forces batsmen on to the back foot out of sheer self-preservation, then slips in a quick half volley – and that gives him a very high percentage of clean bowled and lbw decisions.

Unusually for such a tall man, Joel is not ungainly or unathletic. Most tall men have difficulty in bending or turning quickly but he is a very fine fielder. And because he is not striving for pace – he doesn't have to – he can bowl long spells well within himself, operating uphill or into the wind while a quicker bowler fires in at the other end.

LEFT Wayne Daniel ranks among the six fastest bowlers in the world.
RIGHT Joel Garner's prodigious height, plus a high arm action and a leap in delivery stride means a batsman feels he is facing a bowler on stilts.

LEFT Richard Hadlee – a great bowler because he uses his skills so intelligently.
RIGHT Perhaps not the perfect gentleman but a fine bowler – the enigmatic Rodney Hogg.

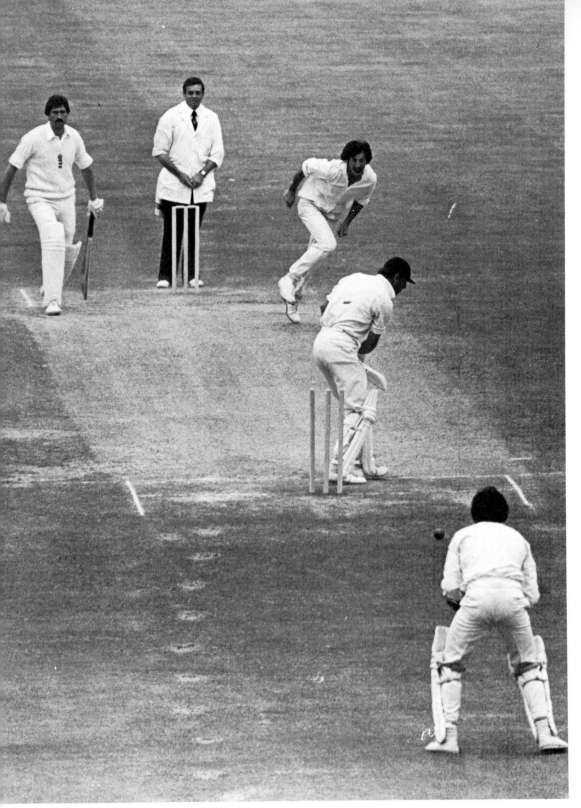

If I had to pick one import guaranteed to strengthen Yorkshire – or any side – it would be Hadlee. Then he could do this sort of thing to somebody else . . .

His hands are huge, which means he can wrap long fingers round the ball and cut it off the pitch, even when the ball is old. Facing him is like trying to combat a golf ball or a brand-new tennis ball bouncing on concrete ... a decidedly awkward customer.

Yorkshire insist on county-born players and quite right too. But if I had to select one bowler guaranteed to strengthen the side – or any side for that matter – it would be the New Zealander Richard Hadlee. His development over the past few years has been remarkable.

Hadlee has always tried to bowl fast, though he is probably a shade slower than the real quicks in the game. He used to spray the ball about a fair bit but now he has learned control, the kind of immaculate control which makes him a truly formidable bowler on any surface.

Even though he does not rate among the very fastest I consider Hadlee a great bowler simply because he uses his skills so intelligently. He has a beautifully economical approach which means he can bowl for long periods, a whippy arm action and the ability to swing the ball prodigiously, even when the shine has gone. He swings the ball away, nips it back, bowls a good yorker and has a very mean bouncer from only just short of a length. All that with a magnificent sideways-on action which takes him close to the stumps on delivery and the ability to bowl straight for over after over. I'm glad there aren't too many Hadlees about but I wish he had been born a Yorkshireman. On our pitches he would clean up the tail without breaking sweat; I could slip off and get padded up as soon as the opposition number eight appeared!

Australia's Rodney Hogg isn't everybody's idea of the perfect cricket gentleman but let nobody doubt his ability as a bowler. He has bags of talent. Rodney is something of a loner and a character. Of course he is temperamental and awkward – there aren't many top-class cricketers who make a habit of kicking down the stumps because they feel they are not bowling well, or demolishing the lot with the bat when an umpiring decision goes against them. But there are plenty of cricketers who feel like doing just that; I've been in the mood for it once or twice though I haven't got round to a demolition job. Not yet anyway.

Rodney reacts. He kicks over the traces. And although I'm not suggesting that petulant behaviour on the field is a good thing, the fact is that the game needs characters and men with character.

For all his histrionics Hogg is an intelligent bowler. He reminds me very much of Brian Statham, bowling a sharp nip-backer and like Statham winning a lot of lbw decisions. But the real beauty of Hogg's bowling is that he hits the sort of length which batsmen hate.

You are never quite sure whether to play forward or back and when a decision has to be made in an instant – Hoggy bowls at a very respectable pace – the law of averages insists that you are going to slip up sooner or later.

It's all a matter of pressure. Facing really fast bowling and especially a lot of short-pitched stuff is one kind of pressure; it's the sort which spectators recognize and

Strength and hostility – Garth le Roux in full flight during the WSC tournament. His prominence there insisted he is a force to be reckoned with.

The one young player in the world undoubtedly destined to become a superstar – the elegant and richly talented David Gower. Don't be fooled by the popular myth that he doesn't care enough about his cricket.

identify with. But facing a bowler like Hogg is pressure too. Back or forward, back or forward, delivery after delivery with Hogg bowling very straight so that the difficult decision always has to be made.

With the new ball Rodney bowls the odd out-swinger; when it gets older he bowls off-cutters and the odd delivery which just holds its line. You tend to get across to cover your off stump and then find yourself cramped for room as the ball nips back. With no space to force the ball away you find yourself playing across the line from gulley to mid-wicket.

A great deal of fuss was made about the fact that Rodney once suffered from asthma and I suspect he plays on it a bit when he fancies a rest. He is rather fond of bowling in micro-spells! But, to be fair, Hoggy discounts the effects of his asthma most of the time and I notice it never seems to bother him overmuch when he is taking wickets. ... When he is bowling he is a determined competitor who often flings himself off his feet in his enthusiasm. Cricket would probably be something of a madhouse if everybody in it was a Rodney Hogg but I like his attitude and his spirit.

South Africa's Garth le Roux still has a reputation to make in English cricket but I suspect that supporters of Sussex are in for something of a revelation before long. The combination of le Roux and Imran promises to be pretty formidable.

Le Roux is tall, strong and hostile. He flourished during last season's World Series Cricket matches and in fact won the Man of the Series Award, based on a points system carrying over from one game to the next. When you consider the batsmen he had to face and the fact that he overshadowed bowlers like Holding, Roberts, Garner, Rice, Procter and Imran it is clear that le Roux deserves a place among the best fast bowlers in the world.

Only a couple of years ago David Gower would have appeared in this book alongside the youngsters with obvious potential for the future. He's skipped a couple of chapters; he had to, because Gower is the one young player in the world who is undoubtedly destined to become a great player – a superstar if you like.

Gower has an enormous amount of natural ability and a very elegant, easy style with superb timing which enables him to play with the minimum of movement. Watching him bat is a bit like seeing a re-run of old cricket matches where the bowler hurtles in at breakneck speed and the batsman still has time to cuff the ball effortlessly away.

David sometimes finds himself in difficulty when the ball turns a good deal or moves significantly off the seam and I think this is because he likes to play with relatively little movement of his feet. He hits the ball with superb timing and a lot of power but he rarely gets his feet as close to the pitch as he might – and that means he is playing slightly on the up, which is not easy on English surfaces.

That may be one reason why he rarely produces as many runs for Leicestershire as his tremendous ability would suggest. County pitches tend to 'do' a bit and his natural style makes David a good pitch player, so I reckon he will become a latter-day Maurice Leyland – a marvellous player destined to average more runs in Test cricket than in the County game.

Batting him at five for Leicestershire is laughably low for a player of his class but the same spot for England does mean that by the time he goes in the ball is not usually new or as lively as it might be. That suits his style and I am sure that Test Matches will become his scene, the arena in which he expresses his talents most attractively.

He is extremely quick, not just over the ground but in terms of relating his eyes, feet and reflexes. He picks up the length of the delivery in a flash and gets into position very quickly indeed. Like many of the great left-handers – and I am bracketing him with men like Gary Sobers, Graeme Pollock and Clive Lloyd – David is not purely a technique player. He has this sense of intuition and inventiveness which is noticeable in the very best left-handers, perhaps as a result of the angle at which they take the ball from predominantly right-arm bowlers.

A lot has been said about his temperament and I suspect David likes the image of the nerveless, ice-cold kid with a cavalier, almost off-hand attitude to the pressures of the game. I think that's something of a façade – and one which troubles some players who would like to see him show more reactions, more emotion.

David rarely registers emotions. Whether he scores a brilliant century or gets out cheaply he preserves this bland, cool exterior, the cricket equivalent of the stiff upper lip. But he cares about his game and cares deeply – let there be no doubt about that. He is no lightweight.

In the first match of England's Australian tour last winter, both David and I were caught at slip, beaten by the left-armer Schuller on a Brisbane green-top. Nets were available later in the day but I didn't go; I felt a friendly game of tennis would do me more good at that particular stage. But I noticed one familiar player in the nets next to the tennis courts – David Gower, quietly working at his game, determined to polish his performance after an early disappointment. Boycott playing tennis and Gower practicing in the nets? Seems that somebody got their images crossed somewhere. ...

6

Young lions

For years England has been bemoaning the shortage of talented young players emerging from County sides to press a claim for Test Match recognition. The Australians exposed the wound when Lillee and Thomson wreaked havoc in Australia in 1974–5, the exceptionally formidable West Indians deepened it with their near-overwhelming superiority in England a year later.

The series against West Indies was dominated by many of the established and richly-talented players who earn their living in our County Championship; compared with them there was a disturbing lack of home-grown talent, or so it seemed.

Strangely enough, our misfortunes then probably did English cricket a great service. It was painfully clear that something had to be done to encourage our best players, and while many people were happy just to complain about the situation – many always are – others stepped in with positive schemes to accelerate the development of the best of English talent.

Sponsors came forward with incentives for young players which had not existed before. Whitbread sent four youngsters to Australia to gain experience and expertise and one of those, Ian Botham, has made a remarkable impact on Test cricket. England already owes a debt of gratitude to schemes such as these, especially when one considers that the sponsors could probably derive more publicity from other fields.

The Counties themselves were jolted into a long, hard look at the English potential available to them and most responded by encouraging young players in their Championship sides. Not all – there will always be some who are committed to winning today rather than planning for tomorrow – but most Counties gave their youngsters a push and with it the opportunity to prove themselves. The emergence of these young players over the last few seasons has been quite remarkable.

Looking round the Counties I see several players who are genuine England prospects. Not simply players with potential but youngsters who have something rather special going for them, players whose talent is all too readily overlooked by those who insist England's cupboard is bare. I shall be disappointed if most of them do not make the grade – and in many cases sooner rather than later. Unfortunately from England's point of view, the majority of exceptional youngsters on their way through are batsmen rather than bowlers. But the best young prospect in English cricket for my money is a fast bowler, Graham Dilley of Kent.

Something of a sensation was caused when he was chosen for England's tour of Australia last winter after barely half a season playing with Kent. That is an extraordinary achievement by English standards; we tend to be far more conservative and cautious than, say, the Australians or the West Indies when it comes to blooding young bowlers at the top level.

But Dilley has the ability to develop and become a real force in Test cricket. He bowls with a slightly chest-on action and I think he always will; in fact I don't think there's any point in trying to change him because he has the strength and temperament to make a reputation as a genuinely fast bowler. Imran and Wayne Daniel bowl chest-on too and I don't remember that slowing them down too much!

A bit of fuss was made in Australia about Dilley's action. He has a pause in his delivery action and that allowed some opportunist Aussie newspapers to suggest he is a thrower. What it does mean is that batsmen find it hard to pick up the length of Dilley's deliveries; the ball comes at you fractionally later than you expect and the delivery you think is a half volley is in fact banging into the block-hole. Graham bowls a very awkward yorker and no wonder.

When he hits his rhythm, Dilley can bowl decidedly fast and I think he will develop quickly enough to surprise a lot of people in twelve months' time. Good players always come on quickly. He looks like a fast bowler with a big, strong frame and a broad backside and from what I saw of him in Australia he has a good, aggressive attitude.

England need fast bowlers of Dilley's breed at the moment. The door is wide open for players like him to force themselves into contention and Dilley has the inbuilt advantage of youth and optimism. No matter how professional a fast bowler may be, the sheer physical exertion of his profession and the wearying repetitiveness of season after season bowling against top-class opposition tends to sap enthusiasm; it's only natural.

Dilley in Australia had all the energy and keenness of a twenty-year-old with a lot to prove. He never seemed to dwell on how hot the weather was, how flat the pitch might be or even how formidable the batsmen were; he just wanted to get on and bowl and that is a marvellous asset for a young fast bowler. He has it in him to carve out a fine future.

Graham also fancies himself as something of a batsman which is no bad thing. He made a big score for Kent last season – 81 against Northants when Kent were in trouble – and he likes to hit the ball hard. A very interesting prospect.

Surrey's Hugh Wilson reminds me forcibly of another fast bowler who started his career with the County and went on to make a name for himself. Tall and gangling and somewhat unathletic-looking, all flailing arms and pumping legs: a striking resemblance to Bob Willis!

Like Willis, Wilson bowls in-swing in the main mixed with a straightish out-

Graham Dilley, the best young fast bowling prospect around.

LEFT Strongly reminiscent of Bob Willis – Surrey's Hugh Wilson. His career might go further if he didn't run so far – forty-three paces really is too much of a good thing.
RIGHT David Thomas of Surrey. A fine prospect who should not surrender his left-armer's ability to swing the ball in search of a yard of extra pace.

seamer. Also like Willis in the early stages of his development, he takes an incredibly long run. It was counted at forty-three paces last season and that really must be too much of a good thing.

Wilson's name was buzzing round the County circuit early last season and a great deal was expected of him. He did not deliver the goods as quickly as some people expected and attitudes seemed to change from optimism about him to carping criticism of his performance. It's not an uncommon circle.

That sort of negative approach to a young fast bowler's development is very short-sighted. If a youngster has it in him to bowl quick – and I believe Wilson has that special something – he should be encouraged to bowl fast and not criticized for lapses in length and line. His priority should be to generate pace.

Most of the great fast bowlers began by concentrating on their ability to bowl at speed; they learned line, length and control as their careers developed but they were never inhibited by the need to plonk the ball on the same spot for over after over. There was no more wayward genius early in his career than Fred; imagine the loss to cricket if somebody had forced him to concentrate on line and length at the expense of his speed. Perhaps we in England tend to be too preoccupied with accuracy; it is obviously essential for medium-pacers but as a philosophy it will not help the production of real pacemen.

Wilson should be encouraged to bowl quick and used in short bursts to nurse his stamina. And I'm sure that somebody should try and sort out that enormous run because I simply cannot see that it is necessary. A bowler's rhythm is a personal thing and only Wilson can really know what kind of run he needs but I would be surprised if he found it genuinely impossible to cut down.

My views on the need to encourage genuinely fast bowlers apply in a reverse sense regarding Surrey's young left-arm seamer David Thomas. Some bowlers have the physique and the aptitude to bowl fast and some don't; I think Thomas has suffered from being asked to bowl too fast in Surrey's search for a really lively pace attack. It was worth trying but I think Thomas is better suited to the lively left-armer's role than that of a genuinely hostile bowler.

When I batted against David last year I got the clear impression that he was wasting his real advantages and talents by trying to bowl too fast. What little he gained – and that really wasn't much – was offset by the loss of the left-armer's dangerous ability to swing the ball into the batsman before cutting it away. Unless he can do both, Thomas will never reach the highest level.

It may be significant that there have been very few really quick left-arm bowlers – in fact you have to go back to Meckiff (could we call that a throwback?) and Voce to find genuine left-arm fast bowlers. The most effective left-armers – men like Sobers, Davidson and Goddard – swung and seamed the ball at a lively fast-medium. They used the natural advantage of the left-armer – angle, swing and control – to great effect.

Thomas has already been on a Young England tour and when he does move the ball he certainly moves it more than most. A fine prospect – but only if he cuts down his pace and learns to swing the ball in as well as cutting it away.

David Gurr of Somerset is a tall, lanky lad who bowled remarkably well for his age during his few appearances with Somerset in 1976. He seemed to lose some of his sting the following season – fast bowlers, like leg-spinners, are notoriously inconsistent when they are young – and a rather unfortunate tour of the Far East with Derrick Robins XI probably didn't help. I am told he lost weight, had quite a bit of stomach trouble and really did not do himself justice.

If he can get himself fully fit and develop his strength, perhaps with a planned course of exercises, Gurr can go a long way. There is no doubt in my mind that he could be one of the brightest prospects in English cricket today.

There is a real danger that Gurr will feel inhibited and overshadowed by the presence of Botham and Garner at Somerset. That is natural enough up to a point but it also means that he must show the character and determination to assert himself – and I sense that he has not got the best out of himself in the last couple of seasons. He seems to have lost some of his appetite for the game. Perhaps it is a false impression but I have an uneasy feeling that Gurr is a little afraid of failure; he fights shy of extending himself in case he falls short in comparison with the internationals in the side. That is a great pity because I feel he has more to offer than most young bowlers if only he can motivate himself to produce his best more often. He was a better bowler two years ago than at the end of last season and that is a very ominous trend. But in the final analysis it's up to Gurr himself; he can either assert himself and make a genuine challenge on the game or he can content himself with being an average County bowler, a wasted potential. I hope he doesn't sit back and slip back.

What Gurr needs now is encouragement, especially in three-day matches as opposed to limited-overs competition. A season's programme of over ninety days is terribly hard work for a young fast bowler, and there is a danger he will burn himself out quickly if he is expected to go flat out in every competition. Far better to encourage him to bowl really quick for seventy-odd days of Championship cricket – he already bangs the ball in from a fair height and generates a useful turn of speed. Pace is probably more important in his development at the moment than accuracy or subtlety; he has time to perfect those and there are plenty of nagging medium-pacers in the game as it is.

Limited-overs cricket can also destroy a young pace bowler's rhythm and give him real problems off a limited run-up. Gurr should be encouraged to think of himself as a three-day fast bowler; he certainly has it in him to develop into the sort of paceman England is always seeking.

Yorkshire's Graham Stevenson has made tremendous strides in the last season or so; he is a good example of the benefits which a winter playing in competitive Australian cricket can bring. When he returned to Yorkshire after five months in Melbourne in 1976–7 he really wanted to play cricket and his character seemed to have broadened considerably.

Stevenson improved dramatically in 1977, so much so that he bowled superbly for two-thirds of Yorkshire's Championship matches. In 1976 he was an ordinary sort of

LEFT Somerset's David Gurr will go a long way if he can assert himself more often.
RIGHT Yorkshire's Graham Stevenson, a young man with star quality who should be encouraged to bowl fast.

LEFT Phil Carrick still has problems to overcome – he must bowl close to the stumps and spin the ball more.
RIGHT David Bairstow, aggressive and entertaining.

three-day bowler and quite a good defender in one-day matches; now he's a very positive attacking three-day bowler who does not switch happily to defensive one day stuff. He obviously finds it difficult to adjust.

Stevenson was awarded his Yorkshire cap in 1978 after a great bowling performance against Lancashire – the sort that makes you realize just what a fine prospect he is. But there's no doubt that he is frustratingly inconsistent and that has tended to hold him back when he should have been making giant strides in the game. The players call him 'Moonbeam' because of the way his face lights up when things go right but he can also become dispirited rather too quickly when the going is hard or luck runs against him. Impressive one day and disappointing the next ... perhaps his nickname is doubly appropriate since there is a theory that South Yorkshire folk are ruled by the moon. Can't vouch for it myself ...

The selectors showed their faith in Graham when they called him into the England tour last winter not so much on the strength of consistently outstanding performances but because they recognized his talent and potential. There is no doubt that if he plays fully to his potential he will not let them or himself down.

Like Gurr, Stevenson needs to be encouraged to bowl quick, to see himself as a strike bowler rather than a line-and-length seamer. Bowling is his strength but he is also a magnificent fielder with a wonderfully powerful arm, very quick on his feet and accurate from the boundary. He sometimes lets his enthusiasm run away with him but he's competitive and aggressive, important in a fast bowler and he's very quick-witted and willing to learn. I can't really see him developing into a technical batsman of any calibre but he is a formidable hitter of the ball, especially over cover and extra-cover. He thumps boundaries over there from off the leg stump which is an amazing feat of strength and timing. On top of all his ability, Stevenson is a crowd pleaser. He doesn't seem to be able to help himself. Whether he is doing something brilliant or just bizarre he has the knack of setting the game alight – and that is an asset not to be underestimated. It is one which will make him genuine star quality.

I have followed Phil Carrick's progress at Yorkshire closely and he is a slow left-arm bowler with real prospects for England, though he has still to overcome one or two weaknesses before we see the best of him. There aren't many slow left-armers around which is a big point – and not necessarily a negative point – in his favour. It means opportunity.

Carrick came to prominence in 1976, found the going more difficult the following season – and learned the hard way that there is no substitute for wickets. Yorkshire gave him his cap after the 1976 season and he thought that would provide enough sense of security to improve his performance, but facts and figures speak louder than a contract of service or a cap with a white rose. That cap also brought greater responsibility – results are expected rather than regarded as an encouraging bonus – and Carrick has found it a hard lesson.

If he is going to bowl really well on better surfaces, the sort he will meet in Test cricket, Carrick must bowl close to the stumps. A couple of seasons ago he tended to bowl from a very wide delivery position with his right foot almost on the return crease, and his delivery angle from there was so wide that when he pitched on middle stump, which would normally be a decent ball, the batsman could work him through mid-wicket because if he missed and the ball did not turn he could not be out.

If he alters his line to bowl a little wider of the off stump he has to be extremely accurate or he gives the batsman room to cut. Those are the greatest sins of the left-armer, to be cut or hit through mid-wicket and when that happens to Carrick it is usually because of this wide delivery angle.

It takes a very fine bowler to bowl well from there and it is impossible for a young man with relatively limited experience to succeed. Carrick has had expert advice from Johnny Wardle and he is the sort of player who will respond to suggestions and tuition.

We also want Carrick to shorten his delivery stride. He is rather spread at the moment of delivery which makes control more difficult and means he does not spin the ball as much as he could. Because he is leaning back rather than bowling from over his front leg, he tends to underspin the ball. Control is vitally important because it helps a spinner counter a batsman who tries to use his feet against him.

He still has problems coming to terms with one-day cricket – and there is no denying the importance of limited-overs stuff at County and International levels these days. Phil wants to play in one-day matches so there's no evidence of any lack of ambition but he seems to lack the confidence to spin the ball; he tends to bowl quicker arm or swing balls at or outside the leg stump. It is not unusual to see spinners amend their style in limited-overs matches but it would be good to see Carrick showing the confidence to bowl legitimate spin.

His batting has improved considerably over the past few seasons and he has played several innings of genuine command and sound technique. He is a good, firm driver of the ball so he prefers firm surfaces where the ball comes on to him; the sort of pitches he would be likely to encounter in the Test arena.

I have dwelt on Carrick's faults partly because I know him so well and partly because I hope he will overcome them. He has the ability to develop into a more than useful batsman, the skill to perfect his art as a bowler and make the grade for England.

Wicket-keepers are a breed apart in cricket. The specialist nature of their role means there is room at the top for only the very best: look how a wicket-keeper of Bob Taylor's ability has missed out on England caps because he was unlucky enough to be a contemporary of Alan Knott. But I see two wicket-keepers in the game who are destined to compete for the elusive England place.

David Bairstow fully deserved his place on England's winter tour of Australia. He has improved beyond recognition since he first played for Yorkshire, a matter of hours after taking his school exams and he has gradually become more shrewd, and more professional in his outlook.

His maturity has shown in his batting, too. He has scored first-class centuries and played several remarkable innings for Yorkshire, small gems in their way. He likes to attack but he has also developed a sound defence and shows a lot of discretion in his innings these days. His naturally aggressive style and speed between the wickets makes him especially formidable in one-day games.

Standing back he is alert and incredibly agile, second to nobody in the game. And when Cope and Carrick began to work well in harness, Bairstow became increasingly proficient standing up. Cope was out of action and Carrick was a learner himself when Bairstow first went into the Yorkshire team and since he had seen few good-class spinners in the leagues he virtually had to start from scratch. A few seasons keeping to a spinner of Ray Illingworth's accuracy would have done him a power of good, but as Yorkshire's spinners have progressed, so he has emerged as a very talented performer behind the stumps.

Like all good wicket-keepers, Bairstow has a profound influence on the team. He is an extrovert – though never to the detriment of his professional performance – full of bounce and energy, always trying to lift the side. There is no better competitor in the Yorkshire side; no matter how difficult the target David always thinks the impossible is possible with a bit of luck and a lot of determination.

He caused quite a stir in Australia last year when he retreated to the boundary because West Indies needed three runs to win off the last ball of a one-day International match. The Aussie crowd had probably never seen anything like it and he came in for some stick, which he took with his usual good-natured sense of humour. It was slightly outrageous but it made good tactical sense and that is exactly what David is all about. He may not be the most aesthetic cricketer but he should never try to be; far better to be himself and let his ebullience and competitiveness carry him through.

Kent's Paul Downton leaped into later prominence when he was selected to tour Pakistan and New Zealand after only seven Championship matches and there were many inside and around the game who questioned the wisdom of the choice. I had never seen Downton before but I watched him on tour and there is no doubt that he has a tremendous amount of ability.

John Murray says Downton has the safest pair of hands he has ever seen on a 22-year-old wicketkeeper and Bob Taylor rates him very highly; they are both top-class players in their own right, judges whose opinion must carry a lot of weight. Certainly, he shaped up remarkably well under trying conditions on tour.

As a batsman he is reminiscent of the young Knott. He is basically defensive which is no bad thing because it is a good base from which to build technique; he likes to play 'inside to out', likes to square drive and to cut. That was just how Knott started and he became the greatest wicket-keeper-batsman in the game. Kent have a tradition for producing top flight wicket-keepers just as Yorkshire don't seem to go without left-armers or opening batsmen for long. With that background and his obvious ability Downton is capable of going a long way in the game.

There are several young batsmen of exceptional ability around the counties and I make no apology for choosing three from Yorkshire. A strong Yorkshire traditionally means a strong England and these are just the sort of players to prove it.

Bill Athey looks every inch a player in the Yorkshire mould of correct, technically

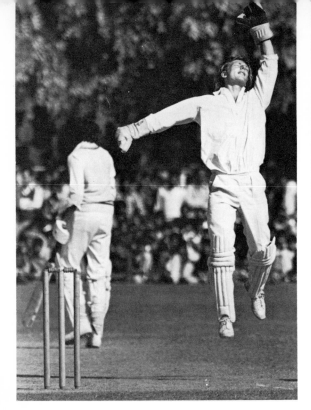

LEFT Paul Downton – highly rated by John Murray and Bob Taylor, and they ought to know.
RIGHT Bill Athey has class and a good temperament, important in a young player who has already
been subjected to a lot of publicity.

Jim Love reminds me of a young Ted Dexter with an upright stance, power and a preference for
hitting the ball in the V between mid-off and mid-on.

accomplished opening batsmen; a bit of Boycott and a hint of Hutton in the way he sets himself and the strokes he plays. He is well-balanced, plays forward and back nicely and has an impressive range of shots for such a young man.

Athey's temperament is sound and that is especially important in his case because he has already been subjected to the fierce glare of publicity. It was too much too soon and like many a young player before him Athey fell into the trap of believing everything that was written about him. He became over-conscious of the Press and that put him under a lot of unnecessary pressure. But he is too talented not to ride that phase in his career and he is bound to come again; his ability to concentrate and the fact that he is prepared to work so hard at his game stamp him as obvious England material.

Jim Love is a very different sort of player but one who can be murderously effective on his day. He reminds me of Ted Dexter – an upright stance, very powerful, loves to hit the ball hard in the V between mid-off and mid-on but can also widen his arc and whip a good length delivery over cover or mid-wicket. Like Dexter he is not a technique player at heart but he has a marvellous eye and is perfectly happy to hit his way out of trouble if the going becomes difficult.

He is a very aggressive character at the crease who does not like to be dictated to. Because his technique is sound he can afford to employ his strength and timing and there are days when it is virtually impossible to bowl at him. He will learn to channel his aggression but it is already a fundamental part of his game and there is no reason why he should change.

Last year was a very testing and frustrating season for Jim, who must have felt that his career had come to something of a halt. He was given few opportunities to play for Yorkshire and the fact that he was dropped after making 170 not out against Worcestershire left him understandably deflated and confused. I feel he could have gone from strength to strength last season and it will be hard for him to pick it up again in 1980; but he should be given every opportunity because he is a player of genuine quality who Yorkshire cannot afford to lose.

Not many people outside Yorkshire had heard of the left-hander Kevin Sharp until he attracted attention by being named as captain of England's Under-19 side against Australia in 1978. His will be a familiar enough name before long.

Sharp is small, deceptively cherubic-looking, a typical left-hander who whacks the ball through the covers and loves to go down the pitch to spinners. Nervous before he goes in to bat, very determined and pugnacious once he gets out in the middle, not afraid to improvise and hit the ball in the air. He is a splendid fielder too.

He will improve technically but his greatest asset is likely to be his wonderful temperament. He is a bright, busy character – the Yorkshire boys call him 'Action Man' because he is always aching to get on with the game – and there is something in his make-up which tells me he is destined to become a star. He simply loves to play and his whole attitude has crowd appeal. England quality, without a doubt.

Middlesex's Mike Gatting made his first England tour to Pakistan in 1977–8 while only twenty and is a player with many sound qualities. At the moment he prefers seam to spin which is not unusual in young batsmen who meet few class spinners in their early years. Gatting drives well through the covers, is alert enough to pull with a high degree of safety and is an exceptional timer of the ball. He hits freely and easily and is extremely strong; perhaps he appears a little on the tubby side but that's muscle, not flab.

Mike has not come on as quickly as it was hoped he would and that may be due to the fact that he has not found himself a settled position in the Middlesex batting order. His natural freedom as a batsman tends to make him a bit loose and vulnerable; I would like to see him settle in at number four and think in terms of controlled big scores rather than quick twenties and thirties.

His ability as a seam bowler will make him a useful player to have in limited-overs competitions but I doubt he will ever make the England side as an all-rounder. He will have to stake his claim as a batsman and if he works hard he has the confidence and quality.

English cricket needs Derbyshire's Kim Barnett to prosper and develop into a Test player. Or perhaps I should say that England needs a player of Kim's type; whether he actually makes the grade is up to him.

Barnett is unique among English County players in that he is a leg-spinner and it's a long time – far, far too long – since we had a wrist-spinner. Australia have always produced leg-spinners and that has gone a long way in giving their Test sides such delicate balance: a leg-spinner who bats is worth his weight in gold.

Kim's batting ability – and there is plenty of it there – is important because with the modern emphasis on quicker bowlers in Test cricket there is little room for anybody who can't bat a bit; and Kim rates higher than that.

He is a hard pitch batsman who strikes the ball on the up and has the overseas player's habit of staying back initially whereas most English players tend to favour the front foot. He's a good cutter and driver of the ball and his batting could develop into a very strong part of his game. In a sense that could become a danger. Because I fear Kim will find, as young, hopeful leg-spinners have before him, that his opportunities for bowling may be far more limited than he likes or needs. It is a fact of cricket life that English conditions favour finger-spinners and although Derbyshire no doubt have a philosophical stake in the future of English cricket they also have to be realistic in their day-to-day approach. Nobody, alas, will thank Derbyshire for blooding and developing a young leg-spinner if their results suffer.

That is a hard fact and there is a risk that Kim will lose his appetite for spinning the ball, concentrate on his batting and just turn his arm over when he gets a chance. That would be a real shame because at present he looks like a genuine wrist-spinner who bats, not just a batsman who bowls funny stuff from time to time.

English cricket should make sure he has every chance to develop. One way of doing that would be to make certain he gets a proper coaching and playing appointment abroad each winter. He could make up in the winter months for his probable lack of bowling during the summer – and the hard, bouncy pitches in Australia would be an enormous help in developing his art.

LEFT Kevin Sharp: bouncy and aggressive, a crowd pleaser with real England potential.
RIGHT Mike Gatting's natural freedom as a player tends to make him a bit vulnerable.

LEFT England need a leg-spinner like Derbyshire's Kim Barnett.
RIGHT Paul Parker, the Sussex prospect who uses his feet against the spinners with uncommon facility. And a brilliant cover-point who anticipates shrewdly.

Kim was in Adelaide on a Whitbread scholarship last winter and that must have done him a power of good. But sponsors naturally like their scholarships to go round, so what will happen to him next winter? I genuinely hope that some sort of scheme can be devised to get him into a good situation abroad again; perhaps another sponsor could step forward and take him on. I'm sure Derbyshire will give Kim all the encouragement they can but I'm also sure that he needs the extra opportunity that winters in Australia can give. He could become an invaluable asset on England's tours abroad, a player who takes more wickets for his country than county. It is vital that he is at least given the chance to prove himself.

After scoring a double century against Essex in 1976 Paul Parker made a century for Cambridge University against Yorkshire and struck me forcibly as a player with a good deal to offer. I was particularly impressed by his quiet, unfussy approach; he began his innings steadily and developed it until he was particularly severe on the spinners. It was uncommon and encouraging to see an English player use his feet so intelligently to make the spinners work. He is aggressive without being a slogger, he plays soundly against seam bowling and varies his game thoughtfully.

Sussex seem to have been trying out a number of youngish players in recent seasons but Parker is a cut above anyone else they have. Apart from his obvious ability as a batsman he is a brilliant cover-point who anticipates shrewdly and is a very quick mover. The selectors obviously have him in mind as England quality; he was awarded a Whitbread scholarship last winter and played in Adelaide.

Chris Tavare of Kent has already scored over a thousand runs in a season and has an uncomplicated, straightforward style which should make him an effective player on good surfaces. My only reservations about him concern a rather inflated reputation early in his career and a tendency to play from a somewhat static position. Tavare uses a long-handled bat which he grips fairly high on the handle and strikes the ball cleanly and hard, mainly through the mid-on, mid-wicket area and through the covers off the back foot. He is not unlike players from Australia and West Indies who like to play 'outside to in'. Tavare is also a superb slip catcher which must count in his favour.

A little bit of Viv Richards may have rubbed off on Somerset's Peter Roebuck, another young batsman who plays commendably straight but also likes to force through mid-wicket. Roebuck has a tall, elegant style and particularly fancies the hook, though he must learn as others have that it is a stroke to be played with the utmost discretion. As a declaration that the bowler is not going to have things all his own way the hook is a perfectly legitimate shot but it is terribly difficult to play well all the time. Once bowlers realize he is likely to hook they will challenge him and he will have to accept the fact that there are surfaces and circumstances where the hook shot is out.

Basil D'Oliviera may have influenced the development of young Dipak Patel at Worcestershire. He is a strikingly wristy batsman who plays through the covers for preference but can cut and sweep effectively. Patel is only twenty-one but has already had a fair amount of experience in County cricket and he is impressively

Chris Tavaré – a freescoring player who likes to play 'outside to in' after the fashion of Australians and West Indians.

LEFT Perhaps a bit of Viv Richards has rubbed off on Somerset's Peter Roebuck, but if he is going to hook as often as he seems to like, he should learn to do it safely.
RIGHT Dipak Patel, impressively mature and composed for a man of 21.

mature and composed for his age. He is a confident and accomplished middle-order batsman who has England material in him. He could even make the grade as an all-rounder since he bowls off-spin with a fine, flowing action and shows good flight and control. He broadened his experience with a Whitbread scholarship in Melbourne last winter.

I regard these seventeen young players as men with the potential of making the England team of the future. Some are more advanced, some already more experienced, than others but they all have talent and the ability to make the grade. With determination and hard work every one has it in him to play for England – and perhaps even the pessimists will then acknowledge that we can still produce some of the finest players in the world.

7

Calling Mr Boycott

Cricket – or at least the kind of cricket which I have known all my career – can never have faced a bigger challenge to its organization or authority than the one which Kerry Packer produced with his plans for a so-called Supertest series.

Every time you picked up a newspaper during 1977–8 the sports pages were full of speculation about which players were going to join Packer's circus, how much money they were going to earn, what effect it would have on county and Test Matches. There were times when we wondered whether the game was meant to be played in the middle or in the corridors of power, real or assumed. Grounds buzzed with arguments about the rights and wrongs of Packer's position; half the world was playing shots and the other half was bowling bouncers. Cricket was somewhere in the middle.

It was not really an argument about whether established cricket was perfect – nobody would claim that – it was more a question of whether Packer's plans would improve it. Like every other sport, cricket has to be prepared to progress and the Establishment has accepted changes in recent years which would have been unthinkable to some of the great names in the game. Changes do not come quickly but it would be unrealistic to accuse cricket of refusing to change.

Everybody who plays sport for a living is something of a businessman; he has to be. It would be naïve to think that goodwill and pleasure in performances, important as they are, represent the be all and end all for the professional. He has to pay bills like everybody else, and goodwill is not very hard currency these days. That is not cynicism, just realism.

However, sport has to maintain a sense of morality or it ceases to be sport. There has to be something more important than money for its own sake, or how can sportsmen hope to keep the respect of the people who pay to watch them play? Packer's plans as they were represented to me meant a lot more money for the most talented and capable players, but not much for the majority of players in the game.

Established cricket, with all its faults, has produced spectacularly good players, men who were welcomed throughout the world because of their reputation, their expertise, the enjoyment they gave to millions. And it says a lot for the character of cricketers in general that most who have done well out of the game – socially and

One side . . . Kerry Packer and Tony Greig arrive for the High Court hearing.

And the other . . . Doug Insole, chairman of the Test and County Cricket Board, the TCCB secretary Jack Bailey and myself.

personally if not financially – have been anxious to put something back. That ensures the continuity of the game; it leaves a thread for later generations to pick up.

These were the thoughts running through my head when I was called to give evidence in the Packer hearing in October 1977. There is something basically intimidating about an English court of law. White wigs, black robes, a strict and mysterious order of procedure with which everyone else seems perfectly at home, the sort of atmosphere which makes you wonder if you have paid the gas bill! I had two days of it, about four hours in the witness box – and that was more than enough considering my most serious brush with the law was a speeding ticket on my way to Edgbaston in the summer of 1977.

The International Cricket Conference and TCCB were represented by Mr Michael Kempster QC, thoughtful and methodical in his approach, a sort of medium-pacer. Packer's case was represented by Mr Robert Alexander QC, a spinner if ever I saw one, alert and wily. I didn't think my innings, part of which is recalled here, was too bad.

Monday 17 October 1977. Examination by Mr Kempster

Q: Have you from your experience on tours any opinion about the amount of time which families should accompany the player, if and when they should, and at what time in the tour?

A: I am not a family man but I wouldn't want children on tour under any circumstances. I think it very pleasurable and proper that wives should come out about half-way through a tour but not for the first six weeks. Players should act professionally, get themselves acclimatized and into good form and practice ready for the Test Matches, which is what they are there to do; they are there to do a professional job. It's reasonable for wives to come out for a short stay about the middle of the tour, then they could go home and the players could carry on doing a professional job.

Q: What responsibility do you feel you have as a County captain to the players in your side as regards representing their interests to the County and the terms under which they are employed?

A: I can't decide myself on anything to do with their finances or contracts but I feel they should come to me with any problems they have and if I feel they have a reasonable point of view it is my duty to go to the County committee and put that view as strongly as I can and see things changed for the better.

Q: Has this in fact happened?

A: Many times.

Q: Tell us about the first time you met Mr Packer.

A: Apparently his boy liked cricket and I was invited to see the boy play in nets in the back yard, to give my professional opinion, as it were. Well, I expressed my opinion, which his father didn't like. We met a second time and Mr Packer said his representative, Mr Austin Robertson, would get in touch.

Q: When you met Mr Robertson was any document produced?

A: Yes, a contract for me to play in Mr Packer's World Series.

Q: Have you still got that document?

A: No, he wouldn't let me bring one away.

Q: Can you recall any provisions in that document?

A: It was virtually, or so I thought, a body-and-soul contract. The terms or remuneration would be approximately $30,000 with bonuses for crowd percentage, royalties and win allowances which teams would share. Also it talked about you could dismiss a player at virtually a moment's notice. I didn't know the legal jargon fully but it didn't seem to me to be very fair to both sides. Also I didn't know until the contract was produced that it was going to be for three years; I thought it was for a one-off period. He said he was coming to England the following summer to sign up players and look for suitable grounds. I said, 'Does that mean I can't play for Yorkshire?' and he said, 'That's right.' I said, 'Hang on a minute, under no circumstances. I can't sign the contract in its present form.'

Q: You know the ICC has amended its rules to preclude from Test cricket any cricketer who was played in a World Series game. Have you considered the reasonableness or otherwise of this alteration in rule?

A: I think they have been over-reasonable. Basically a servant cannot serve two masters. There is nothing wrong in my view with a man going to earn more money from another employer and I said so publicly. I feel that for a long time the leading players in the game haven't been paid what they are worth. But having said that, the two cricket authorities are in direct conflict. The County cricket we play in England depends a great deal on Test Matches, the income which comes in from Test Matches in our own country and abroad. It is split up between the Counties to keep them solvent, to keep cricket going and so provide a breeding ground for young players who will one day play for England. If all this happens it is not going to help English County cricket because the profits are not going to be there from Test cricket. So it seems to me they are wanting the penny and the bun. They are wanting to go away and earn a lot of money in Australia and then come back and play in our County cricket as if nothing had happened.

Q: You also know that the TCCB propose to change their rules to the effect that a player who takes part in a Packer match cannot play County cricket for two years. What do you think of that?

A: I think that is reasonably fair. You have a situation, for example, where a new wicket-keeper from Kent is going on tour with England. If Alan Knott comes back after playing for Packer and is allowed to play for Kent he would take the first team place and young Downton would be in the reserves. That doesn't seem logical; we are not helping English cricket. We will be hindering one of our best young players by putting him back in the reserves after he has been on tour with England, which would seem crazy.

Q: In Yorkshire what provisions do you make for the training and bringing on of players?

A: Really we are affiliated to all the league clubs in Yorkshire and there are literally hundreds. They can send any boy they think has special ability for coaching free of charge. School headmasters can also send boys. We also have winter nets from January through to March where boys in their teens who are of a reasonable standard and have been recommended by clubs and schools can come. They keep a log of the best youngsters round the county and the coach keeps his eye on them and occasionally has summer net sessions so we can still coach them and see how they are getting on. We keep a continuous watch on them until they are just about ready, about eighteen, nineteen or twenty, to play in the second team and then if we feel they are ready and their performance in club cricket is quite good we pick them to play in the second team.

Q: Have you any opinion of a system of cricket which just takes the best cricketers?

A: If a man feels he can earn more money by going away and playing in another country in direct conflict or opposition with the already established cricketers then it is fine for him to do that. He has to earn his living. But he can't come back to the same system that is pouring money in left, right and centre not just to keep a few cream players happy but to keep the whole game going. These players surely can't expect to go and earn a lot of money and then come back and play in the established game. It seems nonsense.

Cross-examination by Mr Alexander

Q: What changes came about when you were capped by Yorkshire?

A: I got a salary, although during the summer when I gave up my job I had had a private conversation with the chairman of the club and told him I had reached a situation where I had to throw in my lot and try and become a professional cricketer or go back and work full time. He said, 'At the moment you are playing full time and getting match fees but if you don't play we will work out some system whereby we will give you so much a week if you are not fit to tide you over the season.' That never arose.

Q: I was reading a book by Mr Illingworth who says in about 1969 Yorkshire never gave their players contracts.

A: That is correct as far as the use of the word 'contract' is concerned. We used to have a yearly agreement. The club wrote to you and said it employed you for a year and specified the salary.

Q: Might the club say to a player, 'We are dismissing you at the end of the month'?

A: No, in my experience with the club it has never done that. It was agreed in the rules – the old rules – that the club had to let you know by the end of July whether they were going to retain you for a further year. When they sacked Brian Close – in my view quite wrongly – it was after July so they still had to pay him another full year, even though he wasn't with the club.

Q: Did Mr Illingworth leave Yorkshire because he wanted the security of a contract?

A: Yes, we did talk about it and I think he wanted a contract for a sense of security. He was getting on a bit but it wasn't just his age. He was being pressured by people who were saying publicly in Yorkshire there is a young off-spinner called Geoff Cope who will be the next world leading off-spinner. He felt he needed the club to come out and say he was the man who should play for Yorkshire; he didn't want them to say, 'We will give you a yearly agreement but next year we will have Cope in and you out' which was fairly reasonable.

Q: Would you agree that County cricketers in general are under-remunerated?

A: We all are except a few overseas stars who get a lot of money. There was an influx around 1969 and for some extraordinary reason they suddenly found another £100,000.

Q: Their introduction was used by other players as a lever to get their own salaries increased?

A: Yes, certainly in my case it was.

Q: In 1974, in your own benefit year, you were actually dropped from the Test side, weren't you?

A: No, sir, I asked to be left out.

Q: Was that because of the strain of the benefit in part?

A: In part, but mainly because I had got to a stage in my career where physically and mentally I had just had enough and I contemplated at one stage giving up the game. I had been playing at the top for several years, I had been on a lot of tours and I was prime target as the leading batsman. A big factor was that I felt the Press was very hypercritical of my performance; they never seemed satisfied with what I did.

Q: You were chosen to go to Australia in 1974–5 and you withdrew?

A: Yes, I went to see Mr Alec Bedser privately and also wrote to him and the Secretary of the Test and County Cricket Board expressing my reasons and explaining what it was all about.

Q: As far as 1972–3 is concerned, did the risk to health in the Indian subcontinent have anything to do with your decision not to be available?

A: I haven't got a spleen, I lost it when I was ten when I had a serious accident and I am concerned that it leaves me more open to germ infection than most. It is something I am very worried about. On the tour to Australia in 1965–6 we went through Ceylon for four days and I was so ill they had to leave me behind in Singapore in hospital. Obviously since then I have been very wary of going to that part of the world; I don't want to get so ill that I end up in a wooden box!

Q: Getting winter employment can be a problem for quite a lot of players, can't it?

A: It has become more of a problem in the last few years. The year when I worked for the Yorkshire Electricity Board there seemed to be quite a lot of opportunities to get jobs for just six months but nowadays it has become very difficult.

Q: Players can hardly take a definite job, can they, if they are hoping to be selected for England?

A: Yes they can, because in my opinion almost every employer who has taken a guy on and finds that he has been picked to tour for England is so delighted for him he says he can go with his blessing. He will say, 'Any commitment you have for me is ended; go and play for your country.'

Q: Players who have given evidence so far say they do well to break even on their coaching jobs abroad.

A: That isn't true. I'm damned sure they make a profit. What they are telling you in court and what they are bandying around when they talk to us in dressing-rooms is totally different.

Q: Are you suggesting they may be fabricating their evidence for the purposes of this court?

A: I am telling you what I know about things that are bandied around. There is nobody who goes to South Africa that I know of and just breaks even. They come home making a profit or some profit they leave in South Africa. As far as fabrication is concerned, you use the word as you want.

Q: When you are playing professional cricket it is hard to build up an alternative career outside the game ... and umpiring isn't really a viable alternative after the game, is it?

A: I suppose it depends on who you are. I personally wouldn't mind umpiring for a year just to see what it's like. I would like to get out a few people who have got me out!

Q: Assume one series for six months only in the Australian summer, no television being transmitted to England and you free to play for Yorkshire. Would you have signed for Mr Packer?

A: Yes, provided I could let my solicitor look at the contract. I wasn't happy with the fact that it seemed to be one-sided. At a moment's notice they seemed to be able to cut you off. Assuming that it was all right I could see no reason not to sign. I was going to play for Waverley anyhow that winter, so I may as well have played in the World Series.

Q: Your attitude would have been if you didn't contravene any rule there was no reason for banning you?

A: Not entirely. I didn't think it was all going to come out as it has done. I thought there was going to be a one-off season in Australia. He said that India were going to play in Australia and they were no good, sort of thing, so he was going to put out one or two matches. And I said, 'Fine.'

Q: Was your attitude one that if the contract didn't conflict with the terms of your registration with the TCCB and your duties to Yorkshire you would have been entitled to sign it without penalty?

A: Yes. I would have expected, though, that I would have been able to go and play for England if I had been selected. It is a normal thing in cricket that whatever County you are affiliated to, your country has prior consideration.

Q: You didn't go on the tour to India last winter, did you? Were you unavailable?

A: Well, it is a moot point.

Q: I can't understand the mootness unless you explain.

A: Officially I had not made myself available but unofficially I had spoken to one of the selectors.

Q: Who was that?

A: Charlie Elliott.

Q: And you had told him you were available?

A: Yes, sir. I told him I was very worried about that part of the world because of my spleen and so forth but I felt I was a bit more fitted physically and mentally to play Test cricket. He virtually said that he didn't think that they would pick me if I made myself available. To put it in a nutshell I said, 'No man is going to take a slap in the face,' so we left it at that. I didn't make myself available officially.

Tuesday 18 October. Cross-examination continued

Q: Would you accept that County cricket with its gates needs all the attractions it can get?

A: No, sir, not entirely.

Q: Are you referring by that to Yorkshire's belief that overseas players are wrong for the game anyway?

A: I am not of the view that overseas star players in County cricket (albeit very nice people and very talented people) does the state of English cricket any good in the long run, because I think they are taking far too many places of English players. At first they would not be as great an attraction as the overseas players but they would learn the trade and eventually England would have a very talented side.

Q: There is no professional cricket in Pakistan. How are these players going to build up their skills in their own countries if they are not allowed to play in this country?

A: From time immemorial these players have built up their skills in their own countries, just as I built up my skills in England before I was selected for England and to go on tours. They do not necessarily have to come to England to be talented players. What England does for them is to add something to their game and give them wider experience of playing under English conditions, which makes it difficult for us to beat them as England.

Q: If Packer players were available next summer there is no reason why the position should be any different from what it was this summer?

A: I am not so sure. Team spirit may suffer a great deal. If the England selectors include Packer people, three or four of the guys that played in Pakistan and New Zealand will not get picked. How would you feel about that? You wouldn't like it, would you; you would get very aggrieved and annoyed about it.

Q: What is the longest contract that you as the country's leading batsman have ever been offered for Test cricket?

A: You are never offered any contract except for the period when you are on tour.

Q: Do you not think the best Test cricketers ought to have more security than that?

A: No. You have to be selected to play in Test Matches as your form warrants it.

Q: In the light of the Packer intervention for the first time Test Match fees have gone up to an acceptable level, have they not?

A: I am not sure that is entirely due to Mr Packer. I am told by an official that negotiations with Cornhill have been going on for some time. I am quite willing to believe they came to fruition a little quicker because of the Packer business and the publicity it got but it had been going on for some time before.

Q: Three-day matches are uneconomical, are they not? If the programme was cut to sixteen three-day matches, that would reduce the loss which County cricket produces, would it not?

A: It would reduce the financial loss but I do not believe it would be good for County cricket. Basically, County cricket is a breeding place for players to become Test Match players. Obviously players have to be paid for playing County cricket but it is a breeding ground and it is not just there as a profit-making business.

Q: The public at large do not go to the County games in very great numbers, do they?

A: That is a bit of an unfair question if I must just answer it 'yes' or 'no'. You have to remember that we at Yorkshire, for instance, have to give enough cricket to 13,000 members who pay twelve guineas a year. It is not sufficient for us to say that the paying public coming through the gate must make ends meet. Some days we play cricket and there are 4,000 people there but we hardly take any money at the gate. We cannot play on one ground; we have to play on nine grounds throughout the county or some members would play hell about it. We must satisfy our members first before we think of the paying customer coming through the gate.

Q: Would you accept that certain people have retired prematurely from the game because they were unable to afford to go on playing?

A: No, I would not say that. I think that those who retired prematurely, like Peter May for example, had basically had enough of the pressure of Test Matches, like I had at the time I mentioned. Enough was enough, they wanted out. I sat down and thought about it and eventually came back refreshed; they opted out altogether and went into other forms of work.

Q: Has your unavailability for Test cricket in the past had anything to do with a belief that you would never be considered for the England captain?

A: No, not really, sir.

Q: You say, 'Not really'. Had that been an element in it?

A: I was disappointed and disillusioned, but it is only a small element.

Q: Did you ask Mr Bedser whether you were debarred for ever from being considered for the England captain?

A: I asked if I would be debarred because it was one of many things on my mind and I wanted to clear up the situation once and for all. Mainly, if I made myself available for England, would they pick me? I was not going to get a public slap in the face. When they chose to pick me was up to them. I also wanted to know for my own peace of mind whether there was to be any bar.

Q: Did you feel previously there were some people who would never forgive and forget?

A: I think there still are. I did feel it previously and I still think there are certain people.

Q: Do you hope that those people may eventually change their minds if the captaincy should ever become free?

A: Yes, I hope they will.

Re-examination by Mr Kempster

Q: In the context of earlier answers about counties like yours which do not take players from overseas failing, perhaps, to contribute to Test sides I would ask you about Hampshire. They play three overseas players, do they not?

A: Yes. Richards, Greenidge and Roberts.

Q: Who do they contribute to the English Test sides?

A: Nobody. I cannot remember them having any in my experience of playing for England.

Q: And Gloucestershire, I think, field Sadiq, Zaheer and Procter. Who have they contributed to the English Test side?

A: Nobody, as far as I can remember.

That was my evidence, or part of it, to the Packer hearing. Since then of course, there has been a High Court ruling, more controversy, fresh developments. The most controversial chapter in the history of cricket and I doubt that we have heard the last of it. But that, as they say, is another story. ...

8

For love or money?

I expect Kerry Packer will probably be remembered as the best thing financially that has ever happened to the top-flight International cricketer. Whether he has done anything for the game itself or the vast majority of players who earn their living from it is another matter altogether.

Packer's intervention undoubtedly brought more money into the game for the top players. The Establishment had been accused of dragging their feet for years, always promising more but invariably coming across with pennies rather than pounds. Then Packer wafted his open wallet and suddenly big money became available for Test players, and not before time.

This does not mean that I have changed my views about the presence of a private promoter in the game; it just doesn't work and cricket can't afford it. Despite what his publicists may claim – and Tony Greig keeps saying, 'I told you so', – in my view Packer did absolutely nothing for the majority of professional cricketers, and he never intended to. Packer did not wade into cricket because he loved the game and wanted to enrich it; he simply saw it as a good business venture which would make money for him and his company.

No doubt Packer and his supporters will point out that all capped cricketers are to receive a minimum wage of around £5,000 in the near future and regard that as a triumph for their claim that his venture would improve the lot of everyone. But the fight for a minimum wage has been fought over several years and the credit for success goes squarely to the Professional Cricketers Association and its advisers. Any benefit which cricketers received – and I can't pretend that top players aren't much better off now – was, I believe, entirely accidental. In fact, since Packer was paying top money to lure players to his World Series Cricket the chances are that he would have preferred others to remain badly paid; it would have made his offers that much more desirable.

I don't think Packer has much professional interest in cricket as a whole, just in that section of it which can be marketed through television for profit. But he made money an issue in the game and it was interesting to see how the Establishment finally got round to accepting sponsorship and trying to project the game more intelligently. It's all very well to see cricket as a pastime played by jolly good sports

The face of controversy.
Unmistakably Kerry
Packer.

WSC logo, cricket's
answer to the skull and
crossbones. It was used
in official limited-overs
Internationals in
Australia last winter.

for the entertainment of jolly nice chaps but it's also somebody's living.

It was also interesting to see how the attitude of the Establishment seemed to change once peace was made and Packer's threat disappeared from the scene. Suddenly there was no money after all, suddenly we had to fight tooth and nail for a realistic wage for the most hectic winter tour an England side has ever undertaken. When they didn't think they had to pay up, the Establishment quickly reverted to a stonewalling attitude; I hope they have more sense than to slip back into the old bad habits, because they could lose a lot of goodwill from the players if they do. Packer succeeded in Australia primarily because the Establishment there had driven the players to the end of their tether – and I hope the lesson was learned.

The Australian Board surprised everybody by announcing a peace treaty with Packer and the suggestion was that he had graciously withdrawn from the game in return for television rights. Nobody who experienced cricket in Australia that winter would believe that for a minute. Packer and the big dollar are still real enough, even to the point where the Aussie Board adopted the World Series Cricket logo – three stumps topped by a red ball – for the limited-overs competition and called it the World Series Cup. And the Aussies seemed to have developed the fixation that anything which Packer cricket introduced must automatically be right.

Night matches themselves were a WSC creation – and a deservedly successful one, I must say – and with them went innovations like white balls, black sightscreens, dark-coloured pads and gloves and coloured clothing. Say what you like about night cricket, it is certainly colourful, even to umpires wearing jet-black clothing during the daylight hours and mustard-coloured jackets at night.

The trouble is that the Australian Board seems to have given Packer everything he wanted and a good deal more. Now that one of his companies, PBL, has been given the right to market the game there is a real danger that Aussie cricket will be run by advertising and media men and not by the Board.

One obvious example of the intrusion of the hard sell in a way which does the game not a ha'porth of good was the introduction of jazzy clothing. Clothing which is a uniform colour has its advantages in night cricket, though the fact that England stuck to white shows it is not absolutely essential. But striped clothing, shirts with contrasting collars and flashes of colour, trousers with military stripes down the side like a jogging outfit, are just so much gimmickry. They may look very fashionable but they don't help the game or make a man a better player, so why bother? I believe that PBL have the right to market the clothing and that they will make quite a lot of money if the kids insist – as kids always do – in having cricket gear the same as the stars? Jazzing the game up in this way is, in my view exploitation.

Let me give another example of the way the game, money and advertising are now bound together in Australia. England accepted a request from the Australian Board to have a team photograph taken to help promote the series and the game. That was fair enough; it's what we were there for after all. But at the same time an agent representing McDonald's, the massive firm with hamburger parlours all over Australia, supervised the taking of pictures (see page 108) which were later given away free with

107

1979/80 INT.
CRICKE

Souvenir Official

AUSTRALIA 1st TEST TEAM (versus West Indies Brisbane Dec. 2 - 5 1979)

WEST INDIES 1979/8

Starting from bottom row, left to right:

Front Row: Rodney Marsh, Bruce Laird, Kim Hughes, Greg Chappell, Alvin Kallicharran, Clive Lloyd, Lawrence Rowe, Deryck Murray, Mike Brearley, Bob Willis, Geoff Boycott, Bob Taylor.

2nd Row: David Hookes, Ray Bright, Allan Border, Michael Holding, Desmond Haynes, Gordon Greenidge, Joel Garner, David Gower, David Bairstow, Derek Randall, Wayne Larkins.

3rd Row: Len Pascoe, Geoff Dymock, Rodney Hogg, Viv Richards, Malcolm Marshall, David Murray, John Lever, Geoff Miller, Graham Dilley, Mike Hendrick.

4th Row: Dennis Lillee, Rick McCosker, Larry Gomes, Derick Parry, Andy Roberts, Peter Willey, Ian Botham, Graham Gooch, Derek Underwood.

Back Row: Collis King, Colin Croft.

Inset
Jeff Thompson

INTERNATIONAL SERIES

rans Photograph

McDonald's

TOURING PARTY

ENGLAND 1979/80 NATIONAL TOURING PARTY

9 SPORTS

every McDonald hamburger. So, without our consent, we were being used to sell hamburgers, not the game as such. And it just so happens that McDonald's are sponsors of a cricket competition in Australia and top television advertisers.

We were really angry about this, angry enough to contact Lord's and ask them to intervene. It may sound a bit trivial but I think the implications were serious; a private company was making money out of endorsements which did the players and the game no good.

Cornhill have put a good deal of money into English Test cricket but I don't think that gives them the right to use any player's name to sell their insurance. And I don't hear Benson and Hedges, who sponsored the Tests in Australia, suggesting that every player was getting through a hundred of their special fags a day.

I think the TCCB could have more strictly controlled how far private firms were able to make money out of the game – but the Aussies seem at the mercy of PBL who market the game in the same way as soap powder. It makes you wonder how long it will be before television takes over the game completely in Australia.

The Aussie Board have certainly thrown themselves wholeheartedly into the marriage, even it if was a shotgun wedding. Ray Steele, Treasurer of the Australian Cricket Board, couldn't bring himself to mention the Packer organization when we were in Australia in 1978/9; he kept referring to 'a private promotor' as though it was an anti-social disease. But towards the end of 1979, at a cocktail function for all the teams and Press, he launched into an attack on the English Press and anyone who dared to suggest that the Australian Board was not completely in charge of the game there, though a child of five could see otherwise.

The Press release of Mr Steele's speech was as follows:

Welcome to you all on behalf of the Victorian Cricket Association and it is especially pleasing to have here tonight with us together for the first time our two greatest cricket enemies, our visitors from England and the West Indies, with both of whom we enjoy a very special love/hate relationship when it comes to cricket. At times over the past few months it began to look as though that love/hate business might be only half right. It is no secret that we have had a few problems recently and of course all sides are entitled to their own opinions about all these matters we have been arguing about – on many we have agreed to disagree – and hopefully all that is now behind us and we can get on with the game. I am personally delighted to see you all here and am looking forward very much to renewing some old friendships and hope that we can all pull together in the interests of the game, forget the past and look to the future.

However, whilst we are all together I do want to take a minute or two, if I may, to get the record straight as briefly as I can, because I believe that it is very important that you, Alec and Ken and Mike and all the members of the England party – and you, Willie and you, Clive, and the members of the West Indies party and the media, at least hear our side of the story – because I don't think it would be any understatement to say that Australia has copped most of the flak over the

Ray Steele: an extraordinary attack on the Press and anyone who suggested the Australian Board was not completely in charge of the game there.

settlement with World Series Cricket. Whether we deserve that or not I will leave to you after you learn a few facts which I think you should know.

Just because everything is not exactly the same as it was before the war there seems to be a tendency to say it is Australia's fault, and there is no doubt in my mind that the public in England are convinced that those Australians have acted off their own bat, without authority, and have sold out to Kerry Packer who now controls cricket in this country, and in selling out they have acquired for themselves a fortune in filthy lucre which they are refusing to share with England and other Test Match playing countries. Nothing could be further from the truth.

Let us go back to the end of last season. World Series Cricket was well entrenched, losing a lot of money but not looking like going away. All the Test Match countries were worried in varying degrees; they had all realized that this was not purely an Australian problem but was truly a world cricket problem, and all countries were being harmed. The WICB of control was insolvent and most of its top players were under contract to WSC. The entire Pakistan team were under contract and the top six Indian players were under option to WSC. They all wanted to see a solution. New Zealand were pressurizing us to try and solve it with the sale of television rights. England wanted a settlement just as much as any of the others. England was not unduly concerned about losing players to WSC but as the only country where cricket is played in the southern winter she could see quite plainly that the financial structure of cricket in England could be threatened if Australia and other countries continued to send teams to tour England which did not include all the best players. All the countries at that stage wanted to see a solution to the problems facing world cricket and we had delegations flying out here from England urging us to do something. I believe that left to ourselves we would probably have continued to fight at least for another season – but this was not to be. We yielded to the pressures put upon us and agreed to try, and I'm glad we did. But don't let anyone ever tell you we acted off our own bat – we did not, and before we agreed to try we took the precaution of getting it in writing, signed by the Chairman of the ICC, that we were not acting unilaterally. I have never seen that published.

You cannot get a solution to a war unless both sides are prepared to make concessions. Certainly we made a few concessions for one-day cricket which I honestly believe were minor concessions taken in the overall concept. Kerry Packer and World Series Cricket made some concessions. You cannot expect to get everything you want. You cannot have your cake and eat it too. We tried hard and it took a lot of time and work. We did our best and finally we got the solution that everyone wanted. We got rid of World Series Cricket.

How can anyone put a value on that? Under our agreement we control cricket, not Kerry Packer, and we control everything to do with the game and we select the teams. WSC has agreed not to promote cricket matches either here or anywhere else in the world. PBL Marketing – they promote and market our programme for us. Sure we conceded things in relation to one-day cricket but not Test cricket.

There seems to be the fear that Kerry Packer is calling the shots. He is not, although I pay tribute to him, Lynton Taylor and WSC for the co-operation and the part they played in the negotiations which led to the solution, and when the chips were down they displayed a genuine concern for the welfare of the game.

There seems to be a fear also that we are denigrating Test cricket in favour of the one-day game. We will never do that. We have programmed six Tests this season and we will always programme at least five or six Tests every season. We have also programmed a limited amount of one day and day/night cricket – far less one-day cricket than is played in England. And if this mix is successful and proves to be what the public want then we will continue to programme that way because I believe we have a duty to give the public what it wants, and Test cricket and one-day cricket are two different games. We committed Australia, but no other country, to experiment in one-day cricket with thirty-yard circles, day/night and a bit of colour. No one is going to be a hundred per cent happy with what we have done, but I believe the concessions we have made are very minor. What is a bit of colour in day/night matches? There is no colour in Test Matches. Some colour is essential anyway if we are to try out the white ball. No doubt we have made and will make mistakes along the way – but so what? – unless you experiment and are prepared to try these things then we will never know what appeals to the public. Whether we like it or not the game has become professional and we are moving into the 1980s, and we must move with the times. No one can hold back change.

Sure we were disappointed that we did not get the co-operation and support we had expected after the agreement was reached, but that is all water under the bridge now and should be forgotten, and I certainly don't want to start it all off again.

But the thing that has really concerned me for some time has been the misunderstanding in the minds of the public. I have been horrified at what my dear old friend Henry Blofeld has been writing these past few months. I had always thought that 'Bloers' had the ear of the Establishment but this time he certainly got the deaf one because he is so wrong in what he has been writing. He claims we 'threw in the sponge', acted unilaterally and let down the side in some way. He accuses us of being 'parsimonious' and of having gone back on our financial promises after England had reluctantly agreed in June this year to make this 'one-off' tour, to do a favour for a friend. Every one of those allegations is not factual and I thought you would have known us better than that and would have known that we don't do those sort of things in this country. Never did we act unilaterally, never did we reduce any financial offer we made by one penny – rather did we increase our offer, and increased our offer again, and this tour wasn't arranged after the settlement. This twin tour with Tests and one-day cricket was part of the International programme since early 1978, not 1979, and it was agreed by the ICC at its 1978 meeting, not its 1979 meeting. The only change that has been made is that the West Indies was substituted for India with the complete agreement of England, India, the West Indies and the ICC, and India will tour here next year. Those sort of things get a bit hard to take, especially the stories that we got a financial bonanza for ourselves. That is ridiculous of course, because both sides lost too much money for it to be possible and in fact we solved the problem at some financial sacrifice to Australia, in the interests of world cricket. The financial terms we agreed were complex and obviously they were commercially acceptable to both sides. I wouldn't be silly enough to try and tell you that they were not commercially acceptable but the only financial bonanza so far is for the TCCB, the WICB of Control and for you, the players. You are all assured of making a lot of money.

We are putting up well in excess of $1 million by way of financial guarantees and we are also putting up in excess of $300,000 in prize money for the players, in addition to your ordinary match and contract payments. Is that parsimonious? Unless the cricket this season 'draws' extraordinarily well we could be looking at another loss and it will certainly be years before we recoup the losses we have suffered over the past two years.

That is all I want to say. Whatever we have done we did because we thought it was in the best interests of world cricket and we did our best. No more thrashing, and this has not been said to cause any embarrassment to anyone but simply in order that at least you have heard both sides of the story. I repeat that it is great to have you all here and I repeat what I have said before, that I believe the settlement is in the best interests of players at all levels, the best interests of the game and the best interests of the public as well. Good luck to you all, and welcome.

It was an extraordinary piece of propaganda and everybody felt rather embarrassed about it, not least the former WSC players in the room. Although Mr Steele has every right to his opinions I don't think he had a right to represent them as factual. There are several points he made which don't bear detailed analysis.

He said the Aussie Board made a few concessions and minor concessions at that! Well, if he calls giving Kerry Packer exclusive television rights a minor concession I wonder what the hell we were supposed to be arguing about for the past two years? If it was that minor why did world cricket become involved in £200,000 worth of litigation? There are seventeen counties in England who look at their bank balances now and don't agree that television rights and everything which sprang from them was a minor issue. A company associated with Packer now has the contract to project the image of the game for ten years – I wouldn't call that a minor concession. If the Australian Board thought the television issue was a minor one they should never have involved world cricket in such a mess. Who did Mr Steele think he was kidding?

Mr Steele made the point that only a limited amount of one-day cricket was programmed in the tour itinerary – true enough as far as it goes. But of course it still presented far more one-day stuff than has ever been undertaken before except in the World Cup which is, I venture to suggest, rather more important than matches designed to make money for a selected band of ICC members. 'Far less one-day cricket than is played in England' said Mr Steele – but not at International level in England where we never normally play more than four Prudential Trophy matches. Mr Steele knows that as well as I do.

Again, Mr Steele claimed that the twin tour in 1979–80 was agreed by everybody concerned in 1978 and he got very upset at the suggestion that the Aussies made their own arrangements. But he knew as he said those words that the original agreement in 1978 was for England and India to play a triangular tournament in Australia, and during this tournament for England to play a few matches in New Zealand; and for England to spend two months in India after the end of the tournament. Not exactly the way it turned out, was it? Sure, a triangular tournament had been agreed – but poor India didn't even take part in it, and who was responsible for that?

And finally, because so much real nonsense has been talked about it already, I must take issue with Mr Steele's remarks about the 'financial bonanza' which the players and the Boards in England and the West Indies enjoyed. Poor Australia, it seems, took part out of the goodness of their hearts and their pure motives have been gravely misunderstood. Well, seventeen Counties in England were to receive approximately £30,000 to share between them, which must be, relatively, the smallest bonanza ever to come out of a series in Australia. The minimum wage for a capped player in England is about £5,000 so I reckon that each County's share of £1,765 would put a little bit into the livelihood of one player at every county. It wouldn't even pay the expenses of a youngster trying to make a start in County cricket. Some bonanza.

Then there is the question of payments to players. Judging by what I have seen reported, I for one was taking my money home in a handcart after the Australia tour. The most ridiculous figures were bandied about and I was supposed to have got well over £10,000. Let's set the record straight, if only for Mr Steele's benefit.

My basic salary was £6,500 and on top of that I received £200 for every previous tour, which added £1,400. That brought the total to £7,900. There were bonuses for winning matches and so on but all of it is subject to tax even if, like everybody else, we get a 25 per cent concession on money earned abroad. So at the end of the tour I reckon I came out approximately £6,000 – hardly the fabulous sums I have seen bandied about. Don't misunderstand me: I'm not complaining and I fully realize that plenty of people would swap places tomorrow. But a lot of hard things were said about greedy cricketers and throw-away remarks about players' bonanzas seem calculated to stir the controversy and hide the facts.

Mr Steele also quotes prize money of $300,000 for the players. If he says so, it must be true. But it would be easy for the public to imagine each team received $100,000, then split that by the number of players and come up with a totally false impression. That figure involved matches between Australia and the West Indies as well as England and Australia. It also included Sheffield Shield and McDonald's Cup matches – so the pay-off was spread considerably thinner than anyone might think, unless you were lucky enough to be the big winners.

The influence of Packer's World Series Cricket was so strong in Australia that their Board, presumably advised by PBL, wanted to play even more one-day games at the expense of Test Matches, which is a fair departure from the traditional Aussie view of cricket. They wanted each team to play twelve matches instead of eight to decide who reached the finals and then spread the finals themselves over five matches instead of three. It appeared to be rampant commercialism and our Board refused, quite rightly in my mind to go so far. From what we could judge, it seemed the Aussies (or was it PBL?) would have been quite happy to play all one-day matches and forget the Tests altogether which would, I think, have been a great disappointment to thousands of traditionalist Australians who still love the five-day games. One-day matches are bigger money-spinners than Tests; you don't have to look far before the profit motive slaps you in the eye again.

And you certainly don't have to look further than the television screen if you watch Channel Nine's coverage of the game. There are advertisements after every over which is bad enough, but the fact that many of the Australian television ads are gratingly shallow and are repeated over and over again during the cricket makes matters worse. It is also common for viewing to be interrupted by running advertisements stripped across the bottom of the screen in print $1\frac{1}{2}$ ins high. Viv Richards is on 99 and you are suddenly urged to buy somebody's used motor cars or that somebody's hamburgers are the best in the world ... it's ludicrous really, but that of course is how the game makes money for the television men.

Because there are so many adverts there is no time for intelligent analysis of the game between overs. Some commentators rattle on endlessly, sometimes breaking off in mid-sentence when the ball is delivered, but there are none of the reflective pauses which English viewers are accustomed to. Perhaps that's the key: English viewers would find the whole thing overpowering and overdone, but maybe Aussie viewers are less critical. Their standards aren't pitched as high; there are too many painstaking explanations to describe the elementary.

Much of the camera work covering the matches is excellent, with an incident replayed from several different angles – though again the Aussies overdo it and show most incidents too often. There are interminable action replays, usually while the commentator tells us exactly what we can see for ourselves. Although England didn't get involved in it, Packer's television has made recordings of player's voices describing how they feel when they score 100 or take a wicket or drop a catch and so on. It might be a good idea but it's pretty phoney, if only because it's obviously not spontaneous.

The actual coverage is good, though the fact that Channel Nine is not national and that many people in outlying areas do not automatically see the matches cannot be good for the game.

Don Bradman, the greatest batsman Australia has ever produced, was born in a tiny New South Wales town and played his early cricket at Bowral, which is no size. Kids in townships like this have television now and it is a great pity that they cannot always watch International cricket on the box: it really would do so much to popularize the game.

Tony Greig fronting the camera for Channel Nine's coverage of International cricket. Yet I suspect he would prefer to be remembered as a player rather than a businessman.

Meals on wheels? Drinks at least – a novel way of saving everyone's feet. Gimmicks like this are increasingly common in the newly-marketed Australian game.

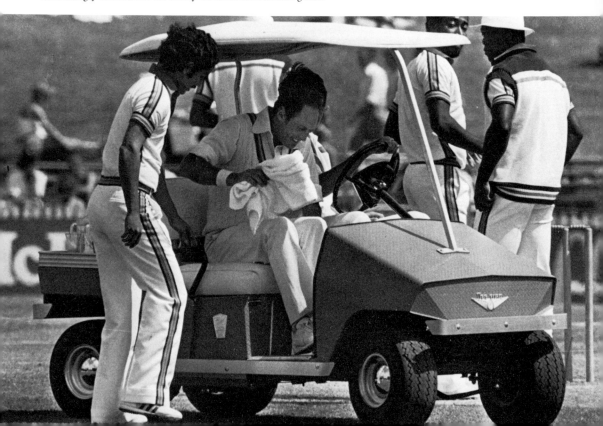

England had only one former WSC player in the squad in Kent's Derek Underwood and there was some speculation as to how he would be accepted by the loyalist players. In practice there were no problems. Most of us know Deadly well enough and although we don't necessarily agree with his views of WSC we don't hold his actions against him personally. Had there been several former Packer men in the party it might have been different; I could easily see a situation where the dressing-room would have been split. But Derek had the good sense not to involve himself in arguments about WSC too much, and we soon got down to the job in hand.

Kerry Packer himself came to a couple of matches but never showed his face near our dressing-room. Tony Greig did, and I had mixed feelings about that, not strictly because of his association with Packer but because he is now involved with the media and I do not believe anyone in that position, even a former England captain, should be given access to privileged information in the dressing-room.

Had I been captain I would have said to Greig: sorry, I have no axe to grind but as long as you are working for the media you cannot come into the dressing-room. We do not allow others in and there is no reason to make an exception for you.

I think Greig is genuinely finding it hard to come to terms with his life outside cricket. In some ways he has got what he always wanted: a good job, a prestigious spot on television and a lot of cash. But he always wanted to be a star cricketer too; he has a big ego and it needs feeding. I think that, given the choice, he would prefer to be in cricket playing for England, and a visit to the dressing-room was the nearest he could come to the old routine. Greig was friendly, seemed genuinely keen that England should win their matches and offered a fair bit of constructive advice and criticism. He felt, for instance, that we should have accepted the proposal to draw circles on the field to prohibit over-defensive play, because our experience and know-how would soon have turned that to advantage. Perhaps.

It would be foolish not to appreciate that some of the spin-off from WSC and the marketing efforts of PBL were exciting and progressive. Night cricket, for example, is a marvellous spectacle, a really atmospheric occasion and anyone who derides it is just being critical for the sake of it. It is a pity that England's climate does not lend itself to the idea of night matches. Mind you, cricket can do without the yobs in Australia who seem only to turn up in droves for night matches – they are like some sections of our football crowds. The public address announcer had a bad habit of not knowing what the winning margin was and, as a result, we would often be blasted out with 'C'mon Aussie c'mon' even when we were playing West Indies! Perhaps it was the only record they had.

Drinks were served to players from a two-man moke which whizzed on to the ground, often threatening to run somebody down. A gimmick, of course, but one which doesn't detract from the game even if it doesn't add much. And another chance to interest a sponsor in the game, which can't be bad.

I liked the way spectators were kept interested during breaks in the International matches by demonstrations of gymnastics, volleyball, soccer and the like. There was

At last – something that makes more noise than the Hill! Somehow I don't see this sort of interval
entertainment catching on at Lord's . . .

a pop group in Sydney and an old-time band in Melbourne, which probably sums up the two cities pretty well, and although it was not possible to please all the fans all the time it was good to see that an effort was made.

The high spot of this extra entertainment for me came during the Perth Test Match when local kids played half a dozen six-a-side matches during the lunch interval. It was a great treat for them, marvellous encouragement at the grass roots of the game which is vital and, last but not least, real entertainment for the spectators. Our players couldn't wait to get out of the dressing-room to watch the matches. Why don't English counties organize something similar? Just imagine the thrill for the kids if some sort of competition was played at the Test Match venues.

The overwhelming desire to squeeze as much money as possible out of the tour – that, after all, is why the whole thing was arranged – involved everybody in too much travelling and too little cricket. The mental preparation for one-day and five-day matches is very different and there just wasn't enough three-day cricket in between to allow players to prepare properly. World Series Cricket had the same complaint in previous years.

Unless the Aussies use their heads I think they may catch a cold next year when India and New Zealand are the tourists and a similar sort of hybrid competition is planned. I can't see the crowds flocking, though they will still be attracted to night cricket – especially if Australia are winning.

The trouble is that a winter tour like 1979–80 devalues the performance of so many good players. It is not possible to turn on top performances to suit the turnstiles and the quality of a lot of games was very patchy, especially the Test Matches. A few more matches up country would have publicized the game more and given players a better chance to achieve and maintain form. It was ridiculous that a player as good as Wayne Larkins should go through half the tour without most people realizing he was there at all ... more three-day matches might have lengthened the tour but they would have given players like Wayne an opportunity to do themselves justice.

Australia expected to make about £300,000 more from the tour than in 1975–6 but that wasn't a great improvement when you consider the increased admission charges and the fact that there were fourteen more one-day matches. With West Indies going strong the triangular tournament involved the world's best so it was always likely to be a success; I fear that the formula will be worked to death and people will soon get sick of it.

9

One day at a time

England were expected to be cannon fodder for Australia and West Indies in the one-day International series in the 1979–80 tour. If the pre-publicity was to be believed – and, to be honest, we weren't over-confident ourselves – the path to the finals was to be strewn with broken English bones and cracked English heads; the finals themselves would be contested by Australian and West Indian sides strengthened by the return of WSC players.

Well, we beat the Aussies and lost to the most powerful side in the world in the finals. But there was a fair bit of argument and negotiation before we even got started. Owing to all the major arguments between the two Boards about the tour, there were a number of points unresolved when we arrived in Australia. It seemed we were expected to accept without question most of the innovations introduced by WSC: coloured gear, artificial restrictions on field placings and the use of a white ball in all one-day matches. Where we considered it was pure gimmickry we put our foot down.

We had never played with circles limiting the number of fielders in the deep and an International series was no place to start, so we rejected that. After practising under lights in Sydney we could see the value of plain-coloured clothing in night cricket as a simple aid to sighting the ball but there was no reason apart from commercialism to accept shirts and flannels from PBL which were covered in stripes and darts. So we turned that down. We could see no sense in using a white ball where no floodlit play was involved, so we rejected that too. The TCCB had already agreed we should use dark pads and gloves to help the umpires give their decisions.

You can imagine how it seemed to the Aussie public: the Poms were whingeing again, wanting all their own way, and Mike Brearley was the 'Ayatollah' who expected his word to be law. It should have been sorted out before we got there and Mike would have been spared the responsibility of spelling out truths which could only make him unpopular – although as it happened the team were behind him in our discussions at the team meetings.

We tried the white ball during day-time matches at Newcastle and even with black sightscreens – which were essential – it didn't have any advantages over the old-fashioned red one. Some batsmen felt it was harder to spot and fielders said it tended to get lost momentarily against the white clothing – so what was the point of using it in day-time?

Obviously it had to be used at night, and that meant it would be used during the daylight innings of day/night matches to make conditions as near as possible the same for both sides. We saw the necessity of using dark pads and gloves and would have accepted coloured clothing of a uniform colour but it was too late to have any made, so we played in white. Some of us did acquire the striped clothing later as a memento (see the photograph on the back of this bookjacket).

We had to play at least four matches under lights and since it was a new experience for all of us except Derek Underwood we approached our first night practices with some misgivings. Our initial impressions weren't too good, especially during the twilight when natural light was fading and the floodlights did not totally restore the balance. We agreed that we would rather bat in natural daylight – the Aussies make no bones about the fact that they prefer to bowl at night – but we discovered as we went on that our misgivings disappeared as our form improved. Perhaps in those early days we blamed our difficulties on the strangeness of playing under lights rather than being simply rusty. By the time the night matches proper got under way our form and confidence had increased and we took to night cricket pretty easily.

The lights in Sydney are magnificent and the atmosphere is tremendous. The white ball does seem to go quicker through the air and it can be awkward to judge during the twilight period, just as speeds and distances are difficult to judge when you drive a car at dusk. It was a matter of adjustment.

One thing we did notice was that the white ball seemed harder than the usual red one. It went off the bat faster and it certainly felt harder in the hands and if it hit an unprotected part of the body. Thigh pad or not, we all had quite a few livid bruises as a memento of night cricket.

There was some concern that the lights might cause problems from reflections in the perspex visors on our helmets but nobody found that a problem in practice. You look through the gap between the visor and the peak of the helmet in any case. I had my visor cut down a bit because the rim was blocking my vision a little against the slower bowlers; it meant the ball could have hit me between the eyes but I trusted my reflexes enough to avoid that.

In fact there were fewer bouncers than most people expected, few casualties and no evidence that the Poms were hopelessly vulnerable to fast bowling as had been suggested. Cannon fodder? It didn't quite turn out that way. ...

West Indies, 28 November 1979, Sydney
I was deeply involved in the first one-day International and I didn't even play. I had been given no hint that I was surplus to requirements but the team was announced with the suggestion that I was a five-day player rather than a one-day. I can't pretend that I wasn't angry and hurt about it. What annoyed me most was the implication that I cannot play one-day cricket. It is one thing to say I am a better three- and five-day player – I accept I am and I don't feel the need to apologize for it – but I am also a

professional who can play one-day games as effectively as most. The records bear that out.

Mike Brearley had to be found a place in the side because he is captain, that is common sense. But I would back myself against him as an opener in any competition known to cricket, so it didn't help my frame of mind to see him walking out in my position while the newspapers announced that I had been left out because I couldn't play the game. The fact that I was not playing also gave the critics another opportunity to suggest I was avoiding the fast bowlers of the West Indies. Sure enough, snide comments were made on Channel Nine by at least one commentator who thought that he knew the *real* reason why I wasn't in the side. The fact that his comments were boringly predictable didn't make them any less annoying.

I was pleased that England had taken three spinners into the game and our use of Miller, Underwood and Willey gave us very important tactical weaponry against West Indies. When Mike Brearley and I discussed the World Cup final I said I thought the balance of the side was wrong and that we bowled the wrong bowlers at the wrong time. From my experience it is pointless to confront the West Indies on form with a battery of pace bowlers; once their adrenalin flows they will simply attack everything and it's almost impossible to slow them down. The important thing was to make them think, to niggle and worry them, plant a little seed of doubt and absorb overs while they were deciding how best to play.

West Indies put us in and Randall and Brearley made a sound start, 79 in 23 overs before Mike was caught out by Greenidge. (Incidentally – and I am not detracting in any way from a useful innings by Mike – I wonder how the Press would have reacted if I had taken 23 overs for 25 runs.)

David Gower made a valuable 44 and Peter Willey hit anything outside the off stump really hard in a great knock of 58 not out. Five is his position and he looks really solid and confident when he's playing well. We finished with 211–8 which wasn't a huge score but could be a winner if we bowled and fielded well.

West Indies looked a bit rusty by their own standards and Dilley and Botham bowled really well in an important opening spell. It was very tight and crucial as far as we were concerned that West Indies didn't get off to a flier. We brought on the spinners in turn and all three had bowled even before Bob Willis got into the attack. It was good tactics and West Indies were never quite in command of the run-rate. We were making them worry.

Fortunately the pitch was slightly in our favour. It was slowish, which meant they could not destroy us with sheer pace, and it turned a bit so our spinners could always keep them guessing.

Even so, West Indies arrived at the last over with nine wickets down, needing ten to win – a hell of a finish to any match. Garner got five off the first four deliveries from Botham, Croft squirted him to third man for two and Bairstow scandalized the crowd (only because they had never seen it before) by retreating to the boundary for the last ball. Botham bowled Croft and England had beaten the world champions.

It was a great feeling, a tremendous sense of elation because West Indies have a

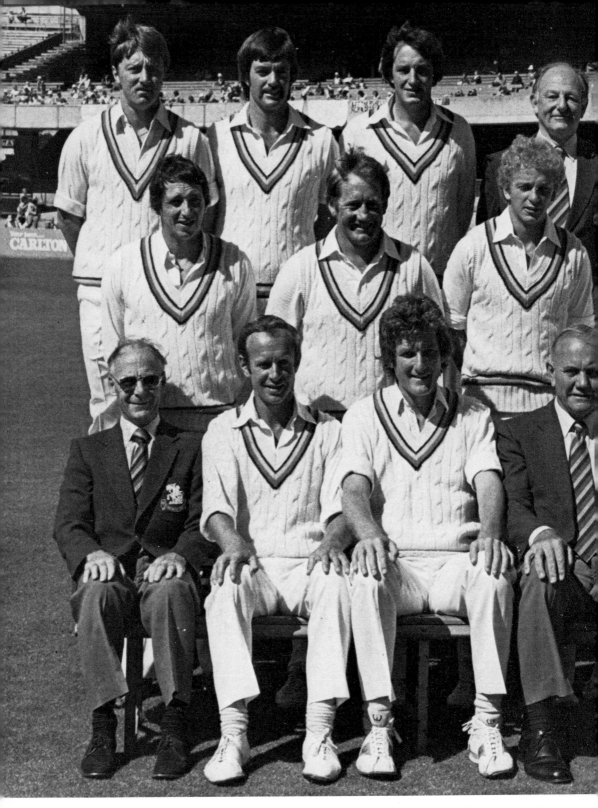

England in Australia 1979–80. *Back row*: Graham Stevenson, Peter Willey, John Emburey, Geoffrey Saulez (scorer), Graham Dilley, Ian Botham, John Lever. *Middle row*: Derek Randall, David Bairstow, David Gower, Graham Gooch, Wayne Larkins, Bob Taylor. *Front row*: Bernie Thomas (physiotherapist), Derek Underwood, Bob Willis, Alec Bedser (manager), Mike Brearley, Geoff Boycott, Ken Barrington (asst. manager).

reputation they deserve for being nearly-invincible in one-day matches. A magnificent finish, and one that will always stick in my memory.

Gordon Greenidge took a great catch to dismiss Mike Brearley, but the one which Derek Randall took to oust Andy Roberts was simply out of this world. Roberts, who had just thumped Underwood for six and could easily have turned the game in favour of the West Indies, smacked another fierce shot through wide mid-on and 'Arkle' soared to his right, caught the ball at full stretch at least three feet from the ground and clung on to it as he hit the ground. There was a prize for the catch of the series and that was undoubtedly the finest catch seen in Australia during that winter.

Australia, 8 December 1979, Melbourne
I made a lot of runs, including centuries against Tasmania and South Australia, before the second one-day match took place. But in view of the result at Sydney against West Indies I wasn't surprised when we announced an unchanged team. The way things were going I could see myself having an extra ten days on the sidelines in place of all the one-day events.

Those who were not due to play in Melbourne had to finish nets by nine o'clock in the morning and then help out those who were. The first time I knew I was to play was when Mike came over at half-past nine and said Geoff Miller was unfit. 'Are you sure you don't want another seamer on that pitch?' I said. 'J.K. Lever could be very useful.' But it had been decided I was to play.

We considered that it wouldn't be the easiest pitch on which to score quickly, so we put the Australians in. Since Greg Chappell was easily their best player our tactics were aimed chiefly at pegging him down. He is a very fine straight player so the spinners bowled as much as possible on leg stump and we tried to keep him away from the strike whenever we could but Greg ran round the spinners and hit them through the mid-off and extra-cover – he only got 92!

The Aussies' total of 207–9 was about 20 runs more than we had bargained for, so we knew we would have to play well. Under the circumstances I was feeling the pressure more than usual.

It was the first time since 1972 that I had faced Dennis Lillee and it was a confrontation that had been eagerly awaited. Australia opened with him and Rodney Hogg, who has got me out a few times in the past; there was 'Tommo' waiting to have a go, and I was playing for my place as the man who wasn't supposed to be much good at one-day cricket.

Once I was in I felt confident. I remember hitting Tommo through cover for four off the back foot; it went like a rocket and I knew I was going to play well. We were in command, the runs were coming and I was enjoying myself so much that after I reached 50 I relaxed mentally and got out to a daft pull shot I should never have played. Normally I can discipline myself to go on once I have made 50 or so but there was something different about that innings – it was as though I had proved myself again and beaten the pressures. I felt pleased with my 68 but slightly ashamed for getting out so foolishly.

A familiar confrontation with Rodney Hogg – and the look on his face suggests that I won this one.

It has been suggested that I played in a way entirely foreign to my nature during that innings but I can't accept that. The strokes I played were orthodox cricket strokes and if I played more freely than on some occasions that was simply because I felt in good form. When I am out of form I find it difficult to get out and that makes my one-day performances look stodgy; when I am in form, as I was in Melbourne I am a good one-day player. I'm sure of it.

Peter Willey played well again but he got out soon after me and we had made the situation difficult for ourselves. From 134–2 we slipped to 148–5 and it eventually needed a fine innings from Brearley to put us back on course. He made 27 when we really needed them and then Bairstow chipped in with a quick 15 to see us home. Bairstow seems to like that kind of pressure; I had no doubts we would win as soon as I saw him strutting out to the middle.

Australia, 11 December 1979, Sydney
I don't suppose I have ever played many better innings than the 105 I scored against Lillee, Thomson and Walker in the second one-day match against Australia. It felt as though a lot of years had slipped off my shoulders and I was playing in the 1965 Gillette Cup final all over again.

I enjoy making hundreds, I enjoy making them well and, most of all perhaps, I enjoy the challenge of making them under pressure. And I was desperately keen to show in Sydney that my innings in Melbourne wasn't just a flash in the pan; I wanted to keep the style and impetus of that knock going and I wanted to show a Sydney crowd that I could play well! Heaven knows they had seen a stilted-looking Geoff Boycott the previous year and I didn't want them to think that was typical.

So I was especially keyed up – and I wanted to be. I deliberately had a net very late so that if we were batting I would feel warmed up and ready ... the lads came over to the nets at 2.15 pm and said we were batting first in fifteen minutes. I had another five minutes, towelled down and changed my gloves. I felt very clear-headed and calculating, motivated by the need to do well, not so much for the critics who still said I couldn't play the one-day game, just for the professional desire to prove myself better.

It all worked out so marvellously well it was like a dream, one of those days you wish could happen every time you go in to bat, but which only comes a few times in a career. 'Tell yourself you are in good form and think positive, you'll get the runs,' said Mike Brearley. We do that every time we go in but it doesn't always produce success.

Mind you it might have been very different. Derek Randall pushed the first ball to Wiener at mid-off, galloped away and almost ran me out! 'I know we want quick singles but that's ridiculous,' I said. Derek just grinned and replied, 'Tha's all right, tha's all right.'

I like batting with Randall because he's quick on his feet and always looking for singles – give or take a suicidal tendency or two. It gets your feet and mind moving, gets you into the game straight away. I didn't get much of the strike in the teens and

The end of a memorable match. David Bairstow and I make a dash for the pavilion after England's heartstopping win in Sydney and Tony Greig presents me with the Man of the Match Award. Not bad for a bloke who wasn't supposed to be able to play the one-day game . . .

drove early in frustration at Walker – Darling was too close because Greg Chappell had brought him in to cut off the singles and dropped it at cover. Big and little innings, praise or condemnation, success and failure are often decided in moments like that.

We skipped along at a fair pace, rotating the strike to keep the bowlers thinking, and after Randall was out Peter Willey again played very well. He considers that because there are no slips and gullies in one-day cricket anything outside the off stump has to go. 'If you can put a piece of wood on it, hit it,' is his motto and it usually pays off for him.

I shall always remember the shot which gave me my century – a four on the up off Lillee through extra-cover. It went so well I knew I didn't have to bother with a run; there was a fielder out there but he might just as well have been sitting in the pavilion.

Inevitably, it seems, there had to be a sour note. I read in a newspaper later in the tour that my gesture of delight towards the England pavilion was some sort of two-finger gesture to the captain and the selectors for leaving me out a couple of matches earlier! Sometimes I despair of such press cynicism. I was proud of myself, elated and overjoyed that England were on top. Who better to share that moment with than the lads in the dressing-room? If I was going to give two fingers to anyone it would be to that pretentious halfwit in the Press box.

David Bairstow blasted Lillee back over his head for six – undoubtedly the best shot of the series to my mind – and we finished with 264–7. It was all over.

The only way to challenge a total like that over 50 overs is to look for about three an over early on, keep your wickets in hands and accelerate later on. It just isn't possible to hit five an over from the start but Australia made the elementary mistake of trying and, inevitably, got out in the process. They were 39–5 after 15 overs.

Two things from their innings hit me forcibly. Doug Walters scored 34 and played our spinners better than anyone in the side, with the possible exception of Greg Chappell. He looked for a run a ball without too much trouble and when the quicker bowlers were on he still looked good because he's a natural leg-side player who can make runs against so-called negative bowling on the leg stump. Doug often gets into trouble around fourth slip and gully but there aren't too many of those in limited-overs cricket.

And Trevor Laughlin, who made 74, hit the ball hard and had the left-hander's inbuilt advantages against bowlers forced to alter their line and length. He can bowl a bit, too, so like Walters he is a very good one-day player.

We never saw either of them again, which was a remarkably blind selection policy from Australia's point of view. Their contribution was forgotten far sooner than the memory of Derek Randall wearing an assortment of caps – including a policeman's helmet – on the boundary edge. There ain't no justice. ...

West Indies, 23 December 1979, Brisbane
Whatever the details, our defeat by nine wickets in Brisbane was frighteningly

simple proof of an obvious fact. West Indies are the strongest all-round side the world has seen for some years. They bat so powerfully that you know you need at least twenty or thirty runs more against them than against any other side in a limited-overs match. Then they bowl so well that it is impossible to find those extra runs ... you are on the horns of a dilemma. When they are playing well there is no way you can escape.

We batted well in Brisbane. Randall, the victim of sudden mental confusion, got out first ball, moving away from a fairly innocuous delivery and sliding it to slip, but everybody else batted well enough to have beaten most teams. The word from the pavilion was that we were looking for 250. Fine, but where from? How do you get above four an over when Holding is bowling like the wind with the new ball and Garner is rattling them round your ribs from his great height. We needed as many runs as we could muster off their reserve bowlers Richards and King (some reserves!) but they conceded 96 off 20 overs which wasn't bad at all from their point of view.

Willey, Gower and Gooch played well, but we gave ourselves up to defeat by trying desperately to lift ourselves to around 250. Perhaps we would have been better off aiming for 230; it often happens like that. We finished 217-8 and it wasn't for want of trying.

Still, we might have had a chance; 217 was a useful total and West Indies had collapsed only two days before against Australia. That meant they had lost three of their four one-day matches and desperately needed a win, which might put pressure on them. Somebody had obviously mentioned all this to Viv Richards. ...

Greenidge and Haynes looked determined enough, smashing 109 for the first wicket in 27 overs. But when Richards came in the whole game exploded round our ears; it was the most incredible display of sheer power and brutal indifference to bowling that you could imagine. I reckon Richards had made up his mind to attack absolutely everything before he faced his first ball. He had made a magnificent century at Brisbane against Australia in the First Test and I think that gave him an appetite to show the locals what he could do, because when he played there in Shield cricket he never really piled on the runs.

So he arrived at a time when the West Indies were winning the match, where the pitch was good and where he felt in top form – and that was the end of the contest. He simply hammered us out of sight; it became the Viv Richards' show with eleven of us tearing about returning the ball so that he could smash hell out of it again. I've never really fancied being a wicket-keeper but I reckon David Bairstow had the best job that day. At least he didn't have to stand in the flight path of Richards' shots – Derek Underwood was quick-witted enough to jump out of the way once – and it's not as though he had too much to do. There wasn't a great deal going through to him by the time Viv finished. ...

Viv's attitude was murderous enough and the heat – an unbearably sticky Queensland day – made it even worse. When I finished batting I stripped down, lay on the dressing-room floor and let Bob Taylor drape wet towels from the ice bucket all over me.

A hot day's work at Brisbane but here's at least one labour-saving device; Deryck Murray follows the flight as I clip a four.

Another shot, another boundary. Viv Richards was in totally irrepressible mood in Brisbane; it was impossible to bowl at him and he virtually beat England on his own.

The attitude of the crowd was extraordinary. They were totally anti-England, booing every time we touched the ball and cheering West Indies on to victory as though it made all the difference to them, which it did not. We expect hostility when we play Australia but this seemed unnatural and quite unnecessary.

Australia, 24 December 1979, Sydney

Australia brought back Ian Chappell and then wasted him by batting him at six. That's my view, at least; it seemed nonsense to me to have Greg Chappell, Hughes and Ian batting at four, five and six in limited-overs competition. If you put your best players down the order in one-day cricket there is always a danger that they won't get in early enough to make full use of their ability. A player like Greg Chappell can dominate the course of any match, so I would give him plenty of opportunity to do it – and Ian isn't exactly a novice! So I would have opened with Ian, batted Greg at three and Hughes at five – splitting the best players to bat in the positions they could do most damage.

As it was, Australia made a very hesitant start, never able to get on top of the bowling. I sensed that after their experience in the previous match they were making a special effort not to lose wickets – and perhaps they overdid such caution. In any case it was left to Greg to pick them up and Ian to retrieve a bleak-looking situation when it seemed they would be lucky to make over 170. Ian is good enough to pick up a run and it's always useful to have a player like that early in the order; he made 60 before the overs ran out (the match was reduced because of rain) by pushing it about and having a bit of a thump at the death.

Australia made 194 but not before Dennis Lillee was involved in some puerile and unnecessary antics, goading Mike Brearley who twice missed a chance to run him out. There seemed absolutely no reason for it, except perhaps a hangover from the aluminium bat controversy in Perth and the suggestion that Mike was getting it all his own way. Whatever points he made, he made on behalf of the team. In my opinion it is wrong for one professional to try to belittle another for whatever reasons. I hope Lillee looks back and regrets his childish and pointless behaviour because a great player like him should not have to resort to such childish tactics.

Australia really needed to win the match and their attitude was obvious even before we went in to bat. At the dinner interval I went for a net to get warmed up. I was surprised to see Hogg, Pascoe, Lillee and Dymock already there bowling themselves loose with the rest of the side fielding the ball; they meant business and that became increasingly evident as the match wore on.

Without doubt, Australia bowled faster and better in this match than in any of the one-day matches we played against them. The quickest – and this may surprise some people – was Dennis Lillee, but all their fast men let it go and gave absolutely nothing away.

Batting was hard work and we weren't exactly helped by a firework display and the roar of speedway engines from the stadium next door. They made a hell of a racket and smoke was drifting across the floodlights, but we had to keep concentrating and

Dejection for Peter Willey after being bowled
by a jubilant Dennis Lillee in a night match at
Sydney.

And a rather more forceful demonstration from
Rodney Marsh, who scythed down his stumps
after being bowled by Graham Dilley.

battle on: there was certainly no opportunity for fireworks on the pitch.

We were just getting on top when Peter Willey got out for 51 – and then there was an almighty collapse. No excuses: Gower, Randall, Botham and Brearley got out to bad shots and I suddenly realized that if I got out we were finished. Hogg picked up three quick wickets, Pascoe two, and it looked as though Australia might do to us what they had done to the West Indies in their previous match.

But David Bairstow knows what batting is all about in situations like this. We needed 16 when he came in and his presence was reassuring. I even hit Lillee over extra-cover, which is not a shot I play every day, and we won with 11 balls to spare. It was a really tense, pressurized one-day match which might have gone either way; the sort of cricket I enjoy, though it was desperately hard work at the time.

Australia, 14 January 1980, Sydney

I don't suppose many people in Australia had actually heard of Graham Stevenson before he burst on them with four wickets and 28 not out in his first International match. I can still see him and David Bairstow running off arm in arm after England's last-gasp win. 'I knew we were in trouble when I saw two Yorkshiremen at the wicket,' said the Aussie tour manager John Edwards later. If the truth be told, he had a lot more confidence in us than we sometimes had in ourselves.

I had injured a hand and could not play, and the fact that we were already through to the finals gave us an ideal opportunity to rest some players and give others a chance they deserved. We had named the same side against West Indies at Melbourne and although that match was rained off there was a lot of loose talk about England naming a reserve side. The 'reserves' weren't going to put up with that.

John 'reserve' Lever bowled magnificently, clearly determined to prove that he should never have been left out of the side and then our off-spinners employed the leg-side theory which Australians hate in principle and can't work out in practice. Australia couldn't get the quick start they wanted and they collapsed hopelessly from 148–3 to 163 all out.

Stevenson picked up four wickets and ran out Dymock and Australia's batting was as confused and misshapen as I have seen from an International side in many a year. It was a complete mess.

The fact is, we weren't much better, with the obvious exception of Gooch, who battled along for 69 in 39 overs while wickets clattered alarmingly at the other end. The crunch arrived when Ian Botham was out for a duck and Bairstow went in with England 61–6. A quick wicket then and it would all have been over, but Bairstow batted with marvellous restraint and commonsense and the score had risen to 105 when Gooch was out. There was still a long way to go but John Emburey thumped a smart 18 and 35 were needed when Stevenson went in.

Lillee was bowling magnificently, a bit piqued, I think, because Thomson and Dymock had been given the new ball. He finished with four for 12 off ten overs, which is the sort of performance likely to win any limited-overs match. But not this one.

Monday night fever . . . Graham Stevenson and David Bairstow gallop off gleefully after snatching victory over Australia by two wickets with seven deliveries to spare in Sydney. Stevenson clinched the win with a subtle boundary – a four over extra-cover off the startled Jeff Thomson!

Gordon Greenidge – key support of the West Indies' team. He liked to attack the new ball and then take a rest when Richards joined him.

Stevenson and Lever were both padded up in the dressing-room and Lever was doing his best to calm Stevo's nerves – at least I think that's what he was doing. 'Look here,' said Lever. 'If we get in together we'll confuse 'em. If I shout "Yes" I mean "No", so don't move. But if I shout "No" I really mean "Yes", so run like hell. …' There was a long pause while Stevenson worked it out. 'I don't know. Sounds ruddy complicated to me. Don't know about confusing them, you've lost me already.'

The lads in the dressing-room put a brave face on it but I reckon they thought we'd had it when Emburey was out. I felt we still had a good chance, not because I'm a complete optimist but because I know how Stevenson plays, and the Australians do not.

Thompson bowls at the off stump; Dymock won't be able to swing the old ball so he'll bowl the left-armer's line at or outside the off stump. Stevenson likes to make room outside the off stump and smash the ball anywhere on that side of the field. Unless the Aussies bowled a leg-side length to him they could be in trouble.

The rest is history. Stevo went marching in trying to stop his knees knocking; he passed Ian Chappell on the way and chirped, 'Nice night for it, innit?' Even Chappell was lost for a reply.

Then he thumped 28 not out off 18 deliveries, including one four off Thomson over backward point which had every Aussie on the ground goggling in surprise. Who on earth was this? He finished the match with a huge four over extra-cover before galloping in with Bairstow, both grinning like Cheshire cats.

Stevenson, as the new boy, quite naturally got most of the praise for England's last-ditch victory and it was ridiculous that he did not win the Man of the Match Award. The panel of journalists making the nomination had to have their votes in half an hour before the end and at that stage Stevenson hadn't even gone in, so it was no surprise they voted for Lillee.

I also think it would be wrong to overlook Bairstow's part in the success. He propped up England for 98 minutes and made 21 priceless runs – without him there would have been no victory for Stevenson to steal against the odds. But we are used to seeing Bairstow play well in tight situations; he has the nerve and the skill to come through time and time again.

West Indies, 16 January 1980, Adelaide

England probably had more going for them in Adelaide than anywhere else on the Australian tour – and we made a complete mess of the match against West Indies. They are a great side, of course, but nearly 25,000 spectators turned up at the Adelaide Oval – and for once most of them were prepared to be on our side. We never looked like giving them anything to cheer.

The pitch was a beauty, the outfield was typically fast for Adelaide and the boundaries square of the pitch are among the shortest in the first-class game. Although West Indies' score of 246-5 was formidable, we should have got somewhere near 200 in reply. We were bowled out apologetically for 139.

Ian Botham bowled well near the end of West Indies' innings but, apart from that, the only time we exerted a measure of containment was when the off-spinners Willey and Emburey bowled. They didn't look like getting wickets – our leg theory wasn't nearly as effective against West Indies, who are natural leg-side players – but at least they kept the scoring in reasonable bounds.

Viv Richards thumped two sixes and six fours in 88 – and ninety per cent of his runs were scored in the area between mid-wicket and backward square-leg. We kept a graph of his scoring shots and decided as a result to use a 7–2 leg-side field for him in the finals, so at least we learned something.

Apart from the sheer inevitability of the West Indies' score, their innings was memorable for a brilliant catch by Botham to dismiss Kallicharran for 57. Kalli drove confidently but Botham, on his follow-through, twisted to parry the ball and then flung himself to catch it one-handed as it looped over his head – a really great catch, fit to rival Derek Randall's in Sydney.

Our bowlers hadn't exactly covered themselves in glory but, as I have said, the pitch was a beauty and West Indies might have plundered any attack for more than 246 in 50 overs. But our batting was little short of pathetic.

Apart from myself, our batting was at full strength and yet we never looked like making any kind of score. Half the side was out for 68 – on a perfect batting pitch – by the time Collis King finished an early burst and then Andy Roberts mopped up the rest. It was a dispirited, feeble attempt at batsmanship which let down the side and those spectators who had gone not only to see an entertaining game but also in the hope that England would do well. It did nothing for morale with three finals against West Indies coming up.

Mike Brearley tried to put a brave face on it by suggesting that there was bound to be an air of anticlimax since we were already in the finals, and that players found it hard to motivate themselves. Well, I couldn't go along with that at all.

The greatest motivator for any professional sportsman is pride in his own performance; if that doesn't inspire him, nothing will. It's very popular these days to talk about 'motivation' as though it's some sort of external force, but the fact is that England suffered from a simple lack of professional application; when most of the players involved had something to prove, if only to themselves. Larkins, Stevenson, Emburey and Lever were playing in only their second one-day International, and none of the batsmen was exactly overburdened with runs. They all had the chance to lift their form and reputation – and what greater motivation could they have needed than that?

West Indies, First Final, 20 January 1980, Melbourne
The only way to beat West Indies – unless they have one of those off-days which afflicts every side from time to time – is to play supremely well yourself and grab the slightest opportunity. England played ninety-nine per cent well in the first one-day final and it wasn't good enough. That is a measure of West Indies' strength when they are playing well. Yet for so much of the first match England were on top – only

by a whisker admittedly, but that is all you need and expect against a side as good as this one.

West Indies made 215–8 and we were 213–6 when our 50 overs ran out; it could hardly have been closer and I reckon the match revolved round three main factors: the bowling of Colin Croft, our misuse of David Bairstow as a batsman, and two run outs just when our innings had caught fire.

We left out Derek Underwood, surprisingly since his reputation is founded on his meanness as a bowler and it had been suggested his place on tour was determined largely by the number of one-day matches. But the selectors felt that West Indies had Underwood's measure so there was no place for him.

I had my reservations about that, because I believe in a variety of slow bowling. John Emburey cost 31 in ten overs and Peter Willey 48, but Emburey had the advantage of bowling earlier when West Indies weren't looking to slog quite as hard. I reckon that if Underwood had played, Willey wouldn't have cost 48 runs bowling earlier and Underwood would have been more economical under pressure.

But our bowling performance was very good. West Indies could not get away and for the first time on tour even Richards struggled – he exchanged a few angry words with Graham Dilley which was a good sign if only because it showed he was frustrated. We had thought a lot about the way to bowl at Richards and decided that length was just as important as the right line, and Dilley bowled magnificently. That plus the use of a 7–2 leg-side field by the spinners restricted and worried him, and he was out for 23 which is nothing by his normal standard.

Gordon Greenidge scored 80 but even that took a long time for him – 42 overs – and that again was because we thought out a plan and bowled well to it. We realized that Greenidge liked to attack the new ball and then have something of a rest when Richards joined him, so we dispensed with our slips relatively early and put a man at deep extra-cover. Greenidge belted the ball hard time and time again without getting it through or even being able to snatch a single; we couldn't really think in terms of getting West Indies out, but we made life really difficult for them. Had Collis King not laid about Willis at the end they wouldn't have got above 200 and that really would have been an incredible bowling performance.

As it was, we knew we were capable of winning the match if we batted well, and at first everything went pretty smoothly. No histrionics, just a good professional performance with runs coming steadily and a feeling that we had our noses in front.

Gooch was brilliantly caught by King but I made runs and then Willey and Larkins played very well, putting on 50 in ten overs without really trying to smash the ball about – a very fine partnership which looked as though it would win us the match.

Then Willey ran himself out looking for a risky second run to Kallicharran, and Larkins was run out soon afterwards by a brilliant piece of opportunism from Desmond Haynes. Instead of progressing smoothly towards a win we were suddenly straining for it with 50 needed off seven overs.

Mike Brearley went in himself and I think he made a mistake. He had pulled us through a tight situation with a good innings in Melbourne before but we did not need runs as quickly then; Mike makes the best use of his limited ability but he has not the power or the flair of improvization which our situation demanded. David Bairstow has both, and if we had sent him in then I'm sure we would have had a much better chance of victory.

As it was, there were only 21 balls remaining in the match when Bairstow went in and he faced only eight of them. He would surely have been better going in earlier when we needed someone with the strength to pierce a defensive field. We needed four to win off the last ball and Mike could only find Clive Lloyd at deep mid-on for two, so the match slipped away despite what had been a very good performance from England.

A special word about Croft. He had not played in previous matches against England but they left out a batsman, Lawrence Rowe, and brought him in to strengthen the bowling. That was a master stroke for more than one reason. First of all, we had banked on scoring most of our runs in the 20 overs bowled jointly by Richards and King; in fact, they only had to bowl ten and went for 64 runs, another ten overs of them and we would have won easily.

Then there was the way Croft bowled. He delivered the ball from very wide of the crease so that it pitched on the stumps but disappeared at least two feet wide down the leg-side – and that meant it was virtually impossible to put a bat on him. The umpires may have been deceived by the fact that the ball pitched in line; whatever the reason, they did not call 'wide' as most English umpires would have done, and Croft conceded only 23 runs off his ten overs. Using Croft in that way and not having to bowl Richards and King too much probably cost us at least 40 runs – and we only lost by two. It was a tactical coup of vital importance.

West Indies, Second Final, 22 January 1980, Sydney
Once they were up in the final series, West Indies became their old near unbeatable selves. The second final was Brisbane all over again. We did not bat badly but we simply could not find the extra couple of runs an over which we needed, and then they batted through with arrogant self-assurance.

We batted first after winning the toss, not just because it was a good pitch but because West Indies had not won a night match batting second and, coincidence or not, we needed every advantage we could muster.

Croft bowled down the leg-side again and got away with it – 29 runs off ten overs without any intervention from the umpires. The only way to get runs off that sort of bowling is to try to hook every ball, and you have to be pretty nippy to do that successfully against a man of his pace!

I managed to get after Richards a bit but he and King still only conceded 57 between them and that wasn't enough as far as we were concerned. Roberts, experienced now if not as fast as he used to be, conceded only 31 and Garner 44. We tried hard enough and played pretty well but four an over was as much as we could manage: they really were the devil's own job to get away.

We knew full well that we had to restrict Greenidge and Richards; if we could get them out cheaply we might even stand a chance of winning the match. But instead of bowling well as we had done in the first final we bowled very poorly at the outset, a wayward line and length, and they got off to a flying start.

Once they were into their stride there was precious little we seemed to be able to do about it. Greenidge was missed three times which didn't help, though to be fair none of the chances was easy. They simply pounded on and on, not as explosive as they had been at Brisbane but confident, clinical and composed – and just as effective.

By the time the innings was half over there was an air of resignation among the England team. We certainly didn't give it away – everybody tried their utmost to the end – but there was that awful feeling that they were going to win again despite everything we could throw at them. That was not defeatism, just realism when faced with the best team in the world and recognizing the form and mood they are in.

10

The Test series

First Test at Perth, 14–19 December 1979

Perth 1979 might be longest remembered for many of the wrong reasons. It was there that Dennis Lillee hurled an aluminium bat thirty yards and interrupted a Test Match for ten minutes. It was the scene of an altercation between myself and Mike Brearley and it was the place where a game was lost that could and should have been saved. It was cold comfort that in scoring 99 not out in the second innings I was to become the third member – Bobby Abel in the last century and Len Hutton more recently were the others – of an exclusive little club of England players who have carried their bats in Tests in Australia.

The extraordinary episode of the aluminium bat won few favours for Lillee but it did little to help England's cause either. His entanglement with the umpires and with the England captain had fired his temper and it was England who suffered. This little drama, enacted in front of his own Western Australian crowd, provided him with all the energy he needed. Eight overs of Lillee accounted for Randall, myself, and Gower and with Dymock chipping in with Willey's wicket the England first innings was soon in disarray at 41 for four.

The aluminium bat episode started on the morning of Saturday 15 December and finished at the end of the month in the wood-panelled committee room of the Victorian Cricket Association with Bob Parish, the chairman of the Australian Board announcing what the English media unanimously condemned as a piece of milk-sop justice. Lillee's action, they said, had been at best a shabby commercial exercise; at worst he had flouted the umpire's authority and brought the game into disrepute. Lillee was given a severe reprimand and that, too, was condemned. It was seen as the judgment of an Australian Board running out of authority and credibility.

Yet, while I would never condone Lillee's outburst, I think I can understand why he acted as he did, and I believe that he was genuinely angry. I used Lillee's aluminium bat the day before the Test and felt that it would require a fair amount of modification before it could even become a saleable product. But that was not really the point. What was significant was that Lillee had gone to some pains to ensure that there would be no objection to his using his metal bat.

I understand he had written to the Australian Board asking for permission to use it

How to publicise a new business venture – and bring a Test Match into disrepute. Dennis Lillee and Mike Brearley discuss Lillee's use of the aluminium bat at Perth.

LEFT That's out. And when the batsman is as formidable as Greg Chappell, it's good to feel the catch settle securely.
RIGHT Mike Brearley falls to Dennis Lillee after their disagreement over Lillee's bat.

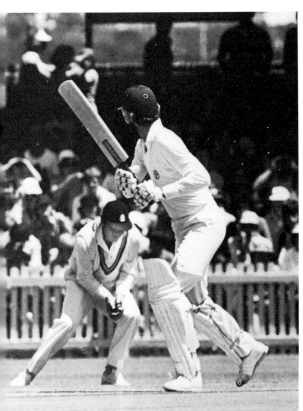

and while they did not exactly welcome it they did not condemn it either.

So having received what he thought amounted to permission to use it Lillee could not then understand why Brearley and the umpires should try to stop him using it, and when he was prevented from using it I think he genuinely felt that he was the victim of an injustice. I think that the Australian Board might have been at fault on two counts. Did they make it clear to Lillee that although they might not have any objection to his using the bat the umpires, being the sole arbiters of what is fair and what is unfair, might have; and did they make an attempt to find out what effect an aluminium bat would have upon a cricket ball?

Possibly the reason that Lillee received such mild punishment was because the Board realized that they were not entirely free from blame. In any event, with new regulations now in force governing the materials that can be used in cricket bats, that is likely to be the last aluminium bat that will be seen on a Test ground.

Although Lillee was furious that Brearley had objected to his using his aluminium bat the Australian bowler, to his credit, did not lose his sense of humour. After dismissing Randall first ball, Lillee walked across to one of the umpires and complained about the tape around my bat. He told him he thought it would damage the ball. As he said this he winked at me, something the umpire did not see. He thought Lillee was being deadly serious and replied with equal seriousness: 'I'm sure it won't. I think it will be all right.'

I thought it was a blunder to omit Gooch from the Test and his exclusion came as a surprise and a disappointment to me as well as to him. I thought, too, that our preparation for the game was far from good. The euphoria that had been engendered by our wins over Australia and West Indies in the one-day games still persisted. Those were matches that we had won when were expected to lose; the more satisfying for that, but then we should have put those games out of our minds. We did not seem to do so and I felt that we entered a crucially important match, the most important in my view, in an untidy frame of mind. That was serious enough. The pre-match practice was worse and it was this that led to my heated words to Brearley.

The importance of the practice was commensurate with the importance of the match. It was vital. Normally, an England side in Perth would have ample time for acclimatisation. They would play a state game which would provide them with most of the knowledge they would require of the pitch; they would be able to practice each morning of the State game and there would still be a couple of days' practice left before the Test.

We had one day on which to get used to a pitch that most Australians would agree is the most difficult in the country. It is also the best because it is the truest but because of its pace and bounce it demands respect. But our attitude to practice was sloppy and unprofessional.

I was tense in anticipation of the Test when I arrived for practice on the Thursday. We had exercises first and then I joined a group taking part in 'nicking' practice – an exercise designed to sharpen catching skills. During the ten minutes that I was there all the catches that went to Botham were dropped. He is an excellent catcher and it was obvious that he was larking about. He laughed a lot and so did the captain. With the Test starting the following day it seemed an unforgivably lackadaisical approach … and a waste of time. I walked off somewhat irritated as I didn't feel the team could afford to waste its practice time. I wanted to get into the nets as quickly as possible.

Worthless fielding practice was followed by batting practice equally valueless. The Australians were using the best nets and I padded up and waited for them to finish. Botham and I were due to bat first, but he did not want to wait for the Australians to finish and, after padding up, moved into a set of vacant nets, which had not been nearly as well prepared as the occupied nets and the ball bounced and seamed alarmingly. It was impossible to play properly and I was livid with Botham.

I wonder what Both would have done if he had then been captain of England. He is an exceptionally talented player and when he puts his mind to it he can show as good a professional attitude as anyone. But too often his reactions have been those of the moment, and lacking maturity. On all the tours I have been on I have never known so much skylarking to take place. There were times when the nets were properly run but too many times when they weren't, and so often Both was the instigator of the frolics.

Our so-called practice meanwhile was wending its merry way, though I confess that I failed to see the funny side of it. When Randall batted Both ran off 21 yards and dug the ball in so hard it soared over 'Arkle's' head, out of the nets, across the road, and disappeared behind some sheds. Botham thought that was humorous; I didn't. What sort of practice is that on the day before a Test? And yet neither the captain nor Kenny Barrington offered a word of reprimand.

By now Gooch was batting and the Australians had finished their practice. I had bowled a couple of balls at Gooch and suggested that we move into the vacant nets and it was no consolation to discover just how good they were. I was furious about the whole thing by now; furious that no one had said anything to Both and furious that my batting practice simply because of Both's impatience, had been ruined. It was at this moment that Brearley asked me if I would go and have a look at the pitch and give him my opinion of it. I gave him a mouthful instead.

It was a thing said on the spur of the moment and born of intense annoyance. Brearley looked stunned, which was understandable because he could not have known what was running through my mind and he could be forgiven for wondering what had prompted such an outburst. I told him what I thought of the sloppy fielding practice and of the poor quality of the nets. Brearley said that this was not his responsibility and it wasn't, of course, but I felt that as captain he was responsible for the way practice was run and that he should have curbed some of the skylarking.

When Brearley asked me to give my opinion of the pitch I told him that there was no need to say what I thought; that I had given my advice before and it had never been taken 'so bugger it'. It was not perhaps one of my most diplomatic remarks but no damage would have been done or embarrassment caused had it not been said within earshot of a local journalist, to whom Mike had been speaking. I did not know that he was a journalist and I feel that Pressmen should not be mingling with the players during practice.

The matter was sorted out between Mike and me and indeed I told Mike that I would look at the pitch, and give him my opinion of it, when I came back for a proper net that afternoon. But the incident was reported in the afternoon editions of the local paper and the story was inevitably avidly pursued by English and Australian Pressmen who were, of course, keen to speak to Mike and to me. But it really was nothing more than a flash of temper, to which, I believe, the majority of cricketers are prone from time to time.

There was a faintly ironic footnote to the story. When Mike asked me to give my opinion of the pitch I also, in anger, told him that I wouldn't be taking any of his catches because I wouldn't be fielding in the slips. But I did field there for a while in Australia's first innings and caught Greg Chappell off Both. A good job I caught it!

One of the few things that was right about the Test was our decision to put Australia in. The ball seamed a lot and we dismissed them for 244, although this total left me feeling less euphoric than some sections of the English Press. There was a lot of deserved praise for Botham, who bowled tirelessly and indeed magnificently, but when you put a side in you are looking to bowl them out for under 200 and on that pitch we should have done so. I thought Australia's total more than useful; they would have done really well if they had reached 300.

The crucial innings for Australia was played by Kim Hughes. He had his share of luck, played and missed, but was in good form. His tour of Pakistan had clearly done his confidence no harm and he struck the ball really hard, much to the pleasure of his home crowd. There were some useful contributions from the tail, too, with Marsh, Bright and Lillee helping to take Australia from 186 for six to 244 all out.

When England batted they met Lillee, still boiling from the aluminium bat episode, in all his fury, but at the end of the innings I agreed with an observation made by Brearley. He said that we had played the Australians, Lillee and Thomson in particular, on their reputations. The pre-match publicity would have had us believe that the pair were so fast they were unplayable and I think that many of us expected far worse than we actually received. Lillee bowled really well but he could be handled; I think we made a mess of our first innings because we feared and anticipated the worse.

We also, it must be confessed, batted extremely poorly. Randall fell immediately to a ball that he simply guided to second slip; I was leg before to a ball that came back, although the bowler must have been able to see all the stumps as the ball nipped back; Willey played an indifferent shot and edged the ball into slips and Gower, not for the first time in his life, was out without using his feet. Miller did not get behind the line of a ball from Thomson and like Willey and Randall steered the ball into the slips while Botham, showing scant regard for the trouble we were in, played an atrocious shot, lifting the ball five feet in the air straight into cover point's hands.

Taylor was bowled by a fairly innocuous medium-paced delivery from Greg

Chappell which came back a little off the seam but easily the two best innings were played by Brearley and Dilley who, in his first Test, acquitted himself extraordinarily well. He battled for more than three hours for his undefeated 38, showing a lot of courage and concentration for someone so young and inexperienced. Mike, too, played a good innings, a spirited, gritty knock. It was as well that this pair batted as well as they did for at one stage we looked likely to fall well short of Australia's first innings total. As it was we finished only 16 runs in arrears.

Australia were given the encouragement of a sizeable opening stand between Wiener and Laird in their second innings but this time the most valuable contribution came from Border, who completed a good hundred. He was struck a nasty blow over an eye as he tried to hook a lifting ball from Dilley but he had scored most of his runs by then and the damage inflicted upon him was not nearly as serious as the damage that he inflicted upon us.

Greg Chappell had been looking for a lead of 380 runs by the last session of the fourth day. He had to settle for slightly less than that, for we were set 354 runs to win in seven hours. More pertinently, we had to bat that length of time to save the game.

England's second innings was, for me, possibly the most decisive time of the tour. I had made nought in the first innings and I was again about to confront a pair of bowlers, Thomson and Lillee, who would be able to operate almost non-stop if required. I was anxious to prove that I could play them as well in Test cricket as I had done in the one-day game and I was under additional pressure knowing I was on the dreaded 'pair' and because people were looking to me to succeed second time round.

I survived the pressure better than I could have hoped, and played as well as at any time of the tour. I did not let reputations disturb me, got stuck into the task from the start, and played almost everything off the middle of the bat. But collectively we batted as badly the second time as we had done the first. It was heartbreaking.

It seemed strange that on the last morning Brearley did not give any instructions to his batsmen. He seemed to take the attitude that there was a job to be done and that everyone knew what that job was. Perhaps they did but they failed to give the impression that they did.

All that was required was to bat all day on a pitch which then was good. It was by no means an impossible task, far from it, one that we should have been able to complete ten times out of ten. And it was simplified by the fact of one man batting all day and facing 50 of the 90 overs bowled.

We made the worst possible start losing Randall and Willey leg before to two big in-swingers from Dymock. Neither offered a shot but their dismissals were at least understandable and forgivable. Anyone can fall to the new ball. What really hurt, and what must have so bitterly disappointed England's followers in Australia and at home, was the wanton manner in which some of our batsmen relinquished their wickets.

Gower's was an infuriating dismissal – a loose shot that clipped a ball from Dymock to mid-wicket. Just before it I had had a word with Gower who had been playing a number of attacking shots. 'You do know that we are trying to save the match, not trying to win it, David' I said. I did not say it cuttingly for I had no intention of telling him how to bat, and no thought of asking him to play like me. But we had already lost two wickets quickly and Gower was playing with the expansiveness of a millionaire. I felt it necessary to make the point that we were trying to save the game. The next over, as if bent on going for runs, Gower was out.

Miller made the same mistake that he made in the first innings, failing to get into line against Thomson and steering the ball to first slip. The first ball that Miller had received he had hit high, off the back foot, through the covers for three. I wondered whether I was beginning to take leave of my senses. What was going on? I tried to advise Miller as I had attempted to advise Gower. 'Look,' I said 'you have just got to settle down a bit. Runs do not matter. Just play steady. Get yourself in.' The next ball Miller steered to first slip.

Botham, either side of lunch, batted with good sense but then his fall was as bewildering and as unnecessary as the others, particularly as we were just beginning to take control. Australia had not taken a wicket for some time when Lillee decided to tempt Both by bouncing him. Both fell for the ruse with a gullibility that in less serious circumstances would have been disarming. He attempted a hook and was caught. There was no necessity to have played the shot. He could have ducked and let the ball go harmlessly by. Time was important, runs weren't. It was beyond me.

Taylor played well for a while and we arrived at tea still with a realistic chance of saving the game, particularly if I could keep an end going. I told Taylor that the first overs after tea could be crucial, that Australia would bowl Lillee for a few overs until he had burnt himself out and then after that it would be easier. Taylor was out to Lillee in the first over after tea, playing on, and after that it was an uphill, and as it proved, fruitless struggle.

We really then had only Dilley left and he tried desperately hard. His performance was all the more meritorious because he had a badly bruised hand, the legacy of a blow received in the first innings. He did well to remain in occupation as long as he did and he set an example of defiant determination that some of the others might with profit have followed. But then he fell to Dymock who, bowling with the new ball, swiftly swept away the last three wickets.

I have often been asked why I did not score a hundred. Surely, people have asked, you could have poached a single from somewhere? I probably could. I might possibly have scored more runs before tea when Australia were waiting for the new ball and bowled the spinners, Bright and Wiener. But if, in searching for a hundred I had attacked the spinners more and got out I might well have been accused of the sort of irresponsibility of which some of the others were guilty.

All the time that I batted I genuinely felt that if just one player could have stayed with me for a reasonable length of time we could have saved the game comfortably. At no stage did I feel that I was going to get out. But I was also lulled into a false sense of believing that somebody would dig himself in and play a defensive innings. But too many players got themselves out just when they appeared to be settling in, and once Dilley had gone the end came so quickly that I had no time to do anything about the situation, I was thus left one tantalising run short of what would have been my 118th first class hundred.

I thought I might have reached it in one of Lillee's overs. I hit a two and then played a shot which should have brought three runs. But Willis had said at the start of the over that he did not want to face Lillee. I asked him why and he replied: 'Because he will get me out.' I don't suppose there is any answer to that but I thought that Dymock from the other end, slanting the ball across the right-hander, represented just as big a threat to him.

I also felt that Willis might have been prepared to run like the wind to give someone who had batted throughout the innings his hundred. I would stress, though, that even at that late and forlorn stage I still had designs on saving the match.

Derek Underwood told me afterwards that when he looked back on the tour and thought of the part that I played in it it would be the innings at Perth that he would remember. It was, he thought, my best performance of the tour. It was an innings I will remember, too, for many reasons and not least because it was almost devoid of false shots. But perhaps most significantly that innings gave the lie once and for all to the accusation, so often aired in the Press, that I had deliberately avoided the world's best fast bowlers, and Thomson and Lillee especially.

Second Test at Sydney, 4, 5, 6 and 8 January 1980

The Second Test at Sydney was effectively won and lost in the only session playable on that first, damp, dismal day when play did not begin until late afternoon. But although Australia beat us again, and in the end by the healthy enough margin of six wickets, we emerged with far more credit than at Perth. We played with the determination and pride that one would expect from an England side.

There were few excuses for the beating at Perth; there was every excuse for this defeat. Whichever side won the toss was almost certain to win on a saturated pitch. The care, or lack of it, given to that pitch amounted to a scandalous neglect of duty. Had such neglect occurred in any other walk of life I believe that the person responsible could have expected the sack.

An unusual amount of rain had fallen on Sydney during the four days before the match. That might not necessarily have been of crucial significance if it had not been for the fact that on New Year's Day all the groundstaff, the groundsman and his twelve disciples, were given the day off, and the pitch was left uncovered. The only explanation I can think of why nothing was said to, or action taken against, the curator was that the Sydney Trust must have given him the day off. If that was so then they were to blame, but even so you would have thought that the curator would have cared enough about his work and taken pride in his job to ensure that at least a couple of members of his staff would be on duty in the event of emergency.

It was scarcely credible. That neglect spoiled the whole Test. Greg Chappell was honest enough to admit even before the game that whoever won the toss was likely to win. It was a lottery even before it had started.

That was not the only controversy. Because of a neck injury, which seemed at first nothing worse than stiffness but gradually worsened, I did not feel that I was fit to play and I was not happy about playing. But when I eventually told the captain that I was not fit to play there was an unholy row and I was ordered to play.

England had prepared for the Test with a game against Queensland at Brisbane. I would have liked to have played in that game but was left out to give others the chance of some cricket. I remained in Sydney resting and playing golf, a relaxing game usually, but the thirteenth at Royal Sydney brought me no luck.

Playing out of a steep bunker I sent up a cascade of sand, half a ton of which went into my eyes. As I climbed out of the bunker my foot slipped and I fell forwards and to my left. I was already half blinded with the sand and as I put my left hand out to save myself I dislocated the little finger. Knowing what to do, I pulled it back into place and thought no more about. But it would appear that that insignificant accident might have been the cause of my neck injury. The following day I woke with a stiff neck and although it got worse I ignored it. I was more concerned with the injured finger which I wanted to ensure was mended in time for the Test.

Brearley and I decided to have a net on the afternoon of New Year's Day. It had started to rain when we arrived at the ground, so I put my pads on quickly and had a knock to see how the finger felt; it was still sore but I could hold the bat without discomfort. I felt then that it would be all right for the Test. Mike watched me bat, waited for me, and I told him that I felt fine.

By the morning of the match, however, my neck was feeling really bad. It had got progressively worse. Bernard Thomas knew about it because the previous night I had gone to the team dinner and on his advice had worn a scarf. He thought I was suffering from a simple, straightforward stiff neck and that a warm scarf would help it. Later, Bernard said he thought I had probably suffered a whiplash injury to my neck when I had slipped in the bunker. I told him that it would be a struggle to bat. I told him that I had better have a net before the start of the match to see if I was fit to play. I didn't think that I was.

I asked Bernard if I should mention it to Brearley but he advised me not to do so. At that stage it did not look as if there would be any play that day. The umpires did not appear to be too keen to see the game start although, as usual, the ground authorities had allowed spectators into the ground, a decision which eventually put pressure upon the umpires to start the game.

Meanwhile, I had gone into the indoor nets with Stevenson and Lever to see if I was fit to play. Willis and Botham came in and stood at the back of the net. They asked Stevenson and Lever if I was fit but they did not ask me. They then left. When I returned from the net I told Brearley that I was not fit to play. Heated words were exchanged and I was practically forced to play.

The Australians did not want to start the match on that first afternoon and in my view they were right. They knew that winning the toss would probably mean winning the match. Brearley surprisingly wanted the game to start, even though we were 1–0 down in the series, because he thought the pitch was fit. He was prepared to take a gamble on the toss knowing that if he won Underwood would almost certainly bowl them out cheaply and England would win the game.

But was it worth taking that risk? If the toss was lost we would almost certainly go 2–0 down and lose the series. I asked Mike if he thought it was worthwhile. He said he thought it was. 'You are gambling with a Test Match' I said to Brearley. 'Surely it would be better to play them on a reasonable pitch and put our faith in our ability.' The gamble failed. Mike lost the toss, and it was no surprise that we were bowled out for a low score.

It might not have been the most vicious pitch ever, but there was little chance of getting any sort of total on it. The main object was to survive for as long as possible and that was not easy. In fact there were two ways of trying to play; try to get a few quick runs or try to survive. Either way it was almost impossible. Gooch and Randall tried to play sensibly but both were out to balls that jumped. I opted for a different approach, playing a few shots and looking to score whenever I could. But I tried to hit a ball from Dymock too hard, and it dipped in and bowled me.

Botham played some good shots, especially a six over long-on off Greg Chappell, and Dilley again showed lots of character and determination, but it was really a case of going through the motions. At stumps on the first day we had lost seven wickets and though there were to be a few twists and turns before the end the game was as good as over.

On the Saturday the pitch had dried a little. It was still damp but nothing like as wet as the previous day. And yet we bowled out Australia for 145. We knew on the Friday night that we were practically out of the contest, but on the Saturday we really got stuck into the Aussies. The bowlers bowled well and the fielders contested every run, chasing and harrying and maintaining the pressure. It was the sort of cricket which had brought us so much success the previous year against Graham Yallop's Australians.

Only Ian Chappell, playing Test cricket for the first time since 1976, batted with conviction. He never looked in danger but allowed his concentration to wander when Gooch came into the attack. He probably thought that he had done the hard work against the better bowlers but in Gooch's first over he drove at a wide ball and nicked it to slip. It was an elementary mistake. If Chappell had not got out then and had built a sizeable innings the game would have been over long before it was. But all credit to Gooch who bowled as well as he can ever have done. He has only three Test wickets to his credit but Gavaskar, Ian Chappell and Marsh are not a bad little haul.

Before stumps we were batting again. The heavy roller was used and the pitch, now losing its moisture, was improving. The ball still moved off the seam, though, and we quickly lost Gooch and Willey. I played well but just before I was dismissed I took a blow on the hand from Pascoe. I could scarcely hold the bat but I was determined to stick it out because it would have been wrong to have expected at that late hour a nightwatchman, or indeed anyone, to have taken my place.

My objective was to try to survive to stumps. There was no pressure on me to score runs and I wanted to reach the close and then hope that the hand would have

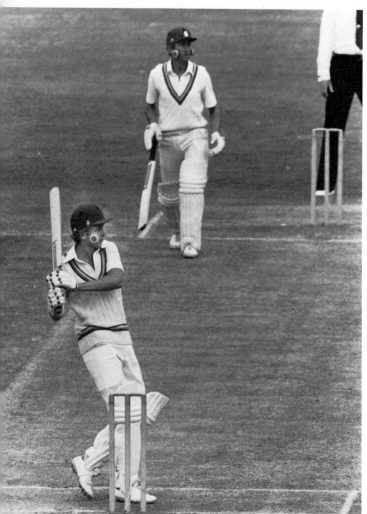

Jubilation for England as Mike Brearley catches Ian Chappell off the bowling of Graham Gooch in the Second Test match at Sydney.

A typically confident shot from David Gower on his way to 98 not out during the Second Test. Bob Taylor looks on appreciatively.

improved by the morning. Unfortunately, completely out of the blue, Pascoe bowled a really quick delivery. The ball seemed to lift from nowhere and although I did my best to fend it off, it lobbed comfortably to gully. I have discussed that ball many times since and I am still certain that there is nothing I could have done to cope with it.

That then had been a day of fluctuating fortune, beginning with our being dismissed cheaply, retaliating really spiritedly to dismiss Australia almost as cheaply, but then losing the initiative late in the day when Australia captured three wickets for 38. I felt that mine was an important one for them for I had made 17 and was beginning to feel that I was getting in.

The third day brought yet another sharp swing in fortune. Underwood had gone in the previous night as nightwatchman and he played the innings of his life. He has done his share of nightwatching over the years, but I think that perhaps he had become a little shell-shocked at having to face the quick bowlers so many times. No one anticipated, or indeed expected, that he would survive as long as he did.

Underwood has done useful jobs in the past, blocking up an end, making sure that he stayed there, but now he went in when we were losing the game and played an innings he will never forget. He is not an elegant batsman, especially when the quick bowlers pitch short to him, as they did frequently that day. He jumps at the ball like a frightened rabbit, face-on with his bat in front of his chest and neck. He sometimes looks as if he will get out every ball. But he has character and determination and does not know when to give up. He batted throughout the morning session, nudging his singles, and making 43 before falling directly after lunch. Underwood's innings would have been outstanding in any game. In this one, on a damp pitch and in a low scoring match, it was priceless. He will not play a better innings in his life.

The other major innings was played by Gower. He was at his most phlegmatic and needed to be on that track. Pascoe beat him time and again outside off stump but Gower could play and miss all day and it would not perturb him. What happened to the last delivery is of no concern to him. Gower promised much before the start of the tour and never fulfilled that promise. But he played really well now.

When Gower arrived we were 105 for five, 83 for five in reality with the 22 runs arrears on first innings deducted, and even after the encouragement of Underwood's batting it looked again that we would lose ... sooner rather than later. But with assistance from Randall he got the score moving again and although Botham and Taylor, Dilley and Willis all fell cheaply he still missed his hundred by only two runs. Willis, sadly, as with me at Perth, was unable to keep Gower company until he reached his hundred.

David deserved his century. It was a splendid innings full of the fluency, charm and timing that we associate with him. Randall, too, deserves credit because he was hit on hand and body but never flinched throughout the morning session. It was a particularly creditable knock because he had had a wretched run of low scores going into the Test and all the confidence had drained from him.

We were all out some 50 minutes before the close and it was a certainty that

Australia, requiring 216 runs, would win, but even then the pendulum might have swung yet again. They were 25 for nought at the close but could so easily have lost Wiener and McCosker; but two umpiring decisions went in Australia's favour. We thought the refusal of an lbw against McCosker off Underwood was inexplicable. McCosker played back to a ball that seemed to be missing leg and missing off but which we thought would have hit middle stump about nine inches up. Underwood claimed that it was the plumbest lbw he had seen in his life. We found it was impossible to know why the appeal was rejected. McCosker certainly did not hit the ball with his bat. And earlier we all thought that Wiener had been caught at the wicket when Willis, bowling quicker than he had done all tour, beat him with a ball that cut back. That was not an easy decision for the umpire but had those appeals gone our way Australia would have been 25 for two instead of 25 without loss and the odds then might just then have been on England to squeeze a win.

The rest day, to our misfortune, was beautiful, and the warm sunshine had dried the pitch into a perfect batting strip. To have any hope of winning now we would have to apply the pressure all day, pray for a couple of early wickets, keep the bowling and fielding as tight as possible and hope that Australia would get themselves into a tangle. The policy worked to a degree but not well enough to deprive Australia of victory.

Fine, tight bowling by Underwood supported by men clustered round the bat gave us the encouragement of two early wickets, with Wiener bowled and Ian Chappell falling to an acrobatic one-handed catch by Both. McCosker played a valuable innings of 41 but even after his dismissal at 98 we might still have won. Once again, however, a vital umpiring decision – probably the most vital – went against us. It was the moment when the Fates decided we must lose.

Greg Chappell was at 32 when he drove at Dilley with his bat a long way from his body. We all felt that he had got an edge as the ball went through to Taylor. Umpire Bailhache was unmoved, but if Chappell had been given out then, as I believe he should have been, Australia would have been 100 for four and with their best two batsmen, the Chappells, gone. Hughes would have been put under severe pressure, and England might have had an even chance of winning. Hughes likes to attack, but at 100 for four he might well have been undecided how best to play and that would have been to England's advantage.

But that is all surmise. Greg Chappell remained and he and Hughes batted with great care until victory was in sight. Then Greg Chappell tucked into Underwood, Willey came in for some severe punishment, and the runs at the end came easily and in a rush, Chappell becoming yet another to miss his hundred by the narrowest of margins, this time by two runs.

England came out of this game exceptionally well. It was a fluctuating contest but one, after losing the toss, that we played against the odds. But we chased Australia right to the end. One never likes to criticize umpiring decisions because sometimes they run in your favour sometimes against, but overall they probably even themselves out. Certainly the decisions went for Australia in this match, and they went in their favour when it mattered most – in the second innings. Wiener, McCosker and Greg Chappell had lucky escapes. If two of those three decisions – or even just the appeal against Greg Chappell – had gone in our favour we might still have won.

Greg Chappell said afterwards that as far as he was concerned the Ashes were up for grabs and Australia had won them. That showed just what the Ashes mean to Australians and I couldn't help wondering if Headingley 1972 was not in Chappell's mind when he made that contentious statement. That was, of course, the year the fuserium disease attacked the Headingley pitch and Underwood, recalled to the England side for his first match of the series, bowled Australia to defeat within three days.

The Australians were bitterly critical of that pitch with some sections of their Press going as far as to say it had been rigged. Gifford had played in the previous three Tests and the Australians thought it deeply suspicious that Underwood should be specifically enrolled for Headingley. Victory there ensured that England would retain the Ashes.

Now the boot was firmly on the other foot. The Australians had produced a wet pitch and England were the victims. But I think that we accepted our defeat with good grace. What else could we do? Whingeing Poms!! Definitely not.

Third Test at Melbourne, 1–6 February 1980

There was some speculation before the Third Test in Melbourne that we might, if we won the toss, put Australia in. There had been an amount of moisture in the pitch on the days before the game but Mike Brearley's decision to bat was vindicated. Gooch and I played exceptionally well, put on 116 for the first wicket and laid the foundations for what should have been a total in the region of 450. It was disappointing that we should fall well short of that figure and bitterly disappointing that our batting overall should, as at Perth, again cost us the match.

The first session went so well for us that Greg Chappell was clearly disturbed. Lillee had bowled with the new ball, failed to worry Gooch or me, and then had retired to the dressing-room feeling unwell. Gooch had kept the score moving by attacking the off-spin of Mallett, stepping down the wicket and hitting him over the top. He had a life when Dymock, at deep mid-off, made a miserable attempt to catch him but that escape concentrated Gooch's mind wonderfully and we arrived at lunch at 100 without loss, easily our best start of the series and the partnership was to become the highest for the first wicket since Brearley and I scored 185 at Hyderabad in January 1978.

When the Australians returned to the field after lunch Chappell gave his men a verbal lashing. He obviously felt that unless Australia improved markedly England could well go on to make the big total that would dictate the course of the game. His sharp words had the desired effect and his bowlers bowled really tightly, making runs difficult to score and thereby putting us under pressure.

I was out to a marvellous catch by Mallett in the gully off Dymock but after

Larkins had made a few steady runs, we were dismissed in the most astonishing fashion by Pascoe and Lillee, who returned from his sick bed and bowled superbly. He bowled off a shorter run at a lively but well-controlled fast medium pace. He was accurate and imaginative, bowling one delivery from close to the stumps, the next from wide of the crease. The man is remarkable. He has the ability to adapt his game to the demands of the situation and he has the capacity to lift the whole team with him. That is the measure of his class.

There was another tenacious innings from Brearley and some valuable knocks from the tail-enders but it was still a poor performance to fall for a little over 300 on that pitch.

Gooch played extremely well, and his innings was a reward for all the hard work that he had put in on the tour. He had trained diligently and kept his weight down for he is a hefty fellow. And now he hit the ball powerfully and straight. But he had himself alone to blame for getting out at 99. Quite honestly, anyone who gets himself out when he is 99 does not deserve sympathy. He had all day to reach his hundred but opted for a dangerous single. He should not have been thinking merely of completing his hundred but of scoring a lot more runs. It was a silly thing to do, born possibly of frustration, because Graham had not then scored a Test hundred.

Australia batted with a solidity unmatched by England. Greg Chappell, truly a great player, made the highest contribution, but there were fine innings too from McCosker, Laird and Ian Chappell. The Australian innings made me wonder whether Derek Underwood was still the 'mean machine' bowler that he was. This match raised doubts as to whether he could come back for a second or a third spell and still maintain his own exactingly high standards. There was only one period when he bowled well, although to be fair to him he bowled marvellously well.

That was between lunch and tea on the third day when he bowled to Greg Chappell. He kept Chappell under pressure, kept him thinking and guessing. It was an absorbing conflict and one that Derek almost won.

Derek had dismissed Greg Chappell a number of times in the past but Greg showed after tea what a great batsman he is, although even such a wonderful player as himself needs a help from fortune sometimes. I think that Greg had decided that he would attack Derek as quickly as possible after tea and try to disrupt his immaculate length and line. Chappell tried to hit Derek over the top and the ball went chest high between bowler and mid-on. It was of a catchable height but went just wide of both for four. The next ball Chappell hit over long-on for four, Brearley immediately put the field back, and from then on Greg was never in trouble again from Derek.

The longer Greg batted the lower and slower the ball became. Some balls went through to the wicket-keeper on the second bounce and yet Greg drove supremely well, especially through extra-cover. His driving was full of authority, arrogant almost. Yet even though he played so brilliantly I thought we erred in our tactics. It was imperative in the circumstances to bowl as straight as possible.

But most of Greg's drives, especially his off drives, came off John Lever, playing in place of the injured Graham Dilley. Now Lever, playing in his first Test of the tour, bowled really well but he was the one player who allowed Chappell the room he needed to play his drives. Bowling left arm over and attacking the off stump meant that Chappell was being given the bit of room he might not otherwise have received.

The ball kept so low that it was difficult to hit. A batsman needed room to get his hands out and away from his body. If the ball went down the leg-side he could move his arms out of the way of his body and flick it away; if it was wide of the off stump he could throw his arms out and drive the ball or punch it square off the back foot. It was very difficult to drive straight with the unpredictable low bounce but Lever's best chance of taking a wicket was to attack off stump but that was also, unfortunately, the line which gave Greg his best chance of scoring runs.

Chappell had dropped himself down the order to six. He was suffering from stomach trouble, a sore throat, and was feeling sick. He was also hampered by an injured leg, ailments which made his innings all the more remarkable. The night before I had remarked to Kim Hughes that Greg had not looked too good in the nets. Hughes said that that was because he was carrying a leg injury, but 'if necessary' he said 'he will bat out there on one leg tomorrow'. He did exactly that.

The low, slow pitch also exposed our lack of a great bowler. We did not have anyone of the class of Lillee, a man who can do things out of the ordinary. We had no one of the pace of Lillee or Pascoe. We had good, honest bowlers but on such a pitch an extraordinary bowler is required. We did not have one. Australia did.

In conditions which encourage swing or movement off the seam our bowlers look of the highest class. They are reared in those sort of conditions. But when the ball does not swing or seam our attack invariably looks plain. Here was a flat, lifeless pitch on which even Botham was reduced to mortal levels. We bowled, or tried to bowl, negatively and waited for the batsman to make a mistake. But the Australians do not make mistakes like we do. On good batting surfaces Australian batting is more safe and sensible than England's.

Australia's tactics after the rest day could possibly have been questioned. They ground on and on throughout a hot day, scoring runs at their own leisurely pace. But I thought their tactics were right. They kept us out in the hot sun for as long as possible and it was demoralising to know that we were really no longer in the game. We should have batted well when we went in again. There was no logical reason not to. But it was no surprise that we didn't. What followed was so predictable. Invariably at cricket the side that is in control gets all the fortune, and that sometimes is all that is required to win the game.

Australia won the Test because of Lillee and Pascoe. They bowled well because they bowled straight. It was very rare that any of their deliveries were off line on a pitch on which the ball was now beginning to creep or shoot or nip back off one of the ever-widening cracks that were beginning to appear. The object for the bowler in these circumstances is to keep the batsman guessing, make him play at every ball, and then hope that the ball will do something strange.

I was first to go. Lillee, unnoticed by me, went slightly wider of the crease and cut the ball back at me. I let it go thinking it would miss off stump. It didn't and I was bowled without offering a stroke. This was good, thoughtful bowling by Lillee and full credit to him but I must have made an uncharacteristic error of judgment or had got my guard wrong. I know that at the time I was feeling tired and had been for three days. I could not seem to summon up any energy no matter how keen I was to bat, and I had so wanted to bat well in that first innings. I was desperately keen to score a hundred.

After three tours of Australia Melbourne remains the only first class ground in the country where I have not scored a century. So I really did try. I do not think the trouble was anything more serious than end-of-tour tiredness. I was in need of a rest. If I am out to a ball offering no stroke I must be in need of a rest.

Larkins was out leg before to a ball that kept low to Pascoe. Then Gower, in spite of the trouble we were in, fell to probably the worst stroke that he can ever have played in a Test. He had no sooner arrived at the wicket than he tried to pull a ball of good length from Lillee. He should have been on the back foot playing defensively and I think the stroke will haunt him for evermore. It was the most reckless of strokes, indisciplined and inexcusable, played when we were trying to save the game.

Willey, who was on a pair, could count himself a victim of misfortune. He played forward defensively, got the thinnest of edges down the leg-side, played the ball on to his pads, which took some of the speed off it, and was caught at the wicket. Brearley was put under pressure with two men, at silly mid-off and silly mid-on, fielding extremely close. Greg Chappell knew his pitch and so did his bowlers. Even when I was batting against the new ball Greg Chappell made do with only two slips, preferring two men in front on the off and one on the leg hoping for the bat-pad catch that one would normally expect off a spinner. But now Greg had men in these positions to the fast bowlers and Brearley gave a bat-pad catch, pushing forward and lobbing the ball gently to Border at silly mid-off.

The Australian bowlers bowled very straight, occasionally dropping one shorter so as to force the batsman on to the back foot; and having forced him on to the back foot they would then bowl a straight, full-length ball which would hit a crack, shoot and somebody else would be back in the pavilion, bowled or leg before. All the while Greg Chappell maintained pressure by keeping men in close, ensuring that the batsmen were kept worrying and wondering about those bat-pad catches. Australia had worked out their tactics well. They knew the Melbourne cricket ground and were aware of the best way to keep pressure on our batsmen.

Botham and Taylor played well to the end of the day but the last day should really have been a gentle, mopping up exercise for the Australians. Things did not, however, work out quite as simply as that. Taylor was out quickly but then Botham played exceptionally well. He blocked the good balls and thrashed the bad ones. There were not too many bad balls but, with his strength and with so many people clustered round the bat, whenever he did he collected four. Lever stayed with him in a stand of 89 for the ninth wicket. Both scored a fine hundred and Australia needed 103 runs to win, far more than anyone could have anticipated at one stage.

Not the grandest feeling in the world – except, of course, if you happen to be Dennis Lillee and another England wicket has fallen in the Third Test.

It's always great to see kids at cricket matches and I don't see any harm in signing an autograph or two while there is an interruption in the play.

It took Australia until well after tea to get the runs which showed how easily we could have saved the game if our batting had been better. Gooch played a second, good innings but was out to an innocuous delivery from Mallett just when he should have been thinking about building a big innings; but a few more innings like Gooch's would have saved the game. The way we batted made Greg Chappell's innings seem all the more extraordinary. He drove the ball beautifully as if he were batting on a perfect pitch. Greg's marvellous batting put ours to shame.

Laird and Ian Chappell played steadily when Australia batted again. The ball kept so low that they found runs difficult to score and they could not force Underwood away at all. The only way Chappell could score off Underwood was to sweep him or to push him to mid-off or mid-on and run like the wind. Underwood showed how scarce runs were to come by if the ball was kept dead straight.

Australia were inevitably going to win but Laird became so frustrated that he tried to hit Underwood over mid-wicket and was caught at mid-on. Runs looked so hard to acquire until Greg Chappell came in again. He had decided that he was going to catch an early plane home to Brisbane. After playing carefully in the early part of his innings he attacked Underwood and gave him some fearful punishment, smiting him to distant parts. Chappell had ordered a taxi for 5.30 pm to take him to the airport, and when the twelfth man tried to bring out drinks at 5 pm he waved him away. Greg was determined to get his taxi and his early plane. He caught both.

II

Conclusion

Mike Brearley was hailed as something of a tactical genius while England were beating Australia in the 1979–80 one-day International series, but we still lost the Test series 3–0 and I think there was a simple enough reason for the contrast in our performances.

Mike is a very competent captain but certainly no genius. We won our one-day matches against Australia partly because they are so inept at the tactics of the game – they certainly don't seem to have learned too much from their limited-overs experience with WSC.

Ability can sometimes be held in check by using the right tactics in the one-day game; that's why matches can be won and lost if only one or two players get decent scores. Viv Richards and Gordon Greenidge did it for West Indies, I did it for England with Peter Willey and Graham Gooch chipping in so we made decent totals.

As far as bowling in limited-overs matches is concerned, it's not absolutely vital to have the best or fastest bowlers at your disposal; after attacking with the new ball what the bowlers have to do is bowl to their field, maintain a good line and length and let the batsmen make mistakes. That's the name of the game.

We learned this in England years ago and the tactics Mike employed were no more than any County captain would have used. Because the Aussies hadn't seen these tactics before and because they wanted some excuse for failure they talked rather a lot of rubbish about magic captaincy.

Australia never paced their batting properly, putting themselves under pressure by trying to go too fast or dawdling along, and they played their two best batsmen – Greg Chappell and Kim Hughes – too far down the order. They are the sort of players who can dominate and direct a match, but by the time they got in too many overs had disappeared or too many wickets fallen, making it difficult to regain the initiative.

Bob Willis was a good example of the way our bowlers used their limited-overs experience. He had lost half a yard of pace but he never made the mistake of trying to bowl too fast or strain for speed alone. He bowled a negative line and length and let the batsmen make mistakes. The Aussie mentality has always favoured the obvious – big fast bowlers and batsmen who like to thump the ball around, aggressive leg-

A thoughtful moment in Perth. Can't remember offhand what I was thinking but no doubt Mike
Brearley was mentally humming a classical tune . . .

spinners – but the one-day game isn't necessarily dominated by simple ability alone.

Test Matches are very different and so were our results. The good players have time to build an innings and bowlers need to be positive and aggressive, the sort of men who can take wickets however unfavourable the conditions or however well the opposition are batting. Australia had better players in better form than we did and when it came to the crunch we were always struggling.

The loss of Mike Hendrick was a massive blow, a lot bigger than many people realize. Hendo is not a star bowler so perhaps his absence was underestimated – had Australia lost Dennis Lillee, for instance, the whole world would have recognized that they were playing under a huge disadvantage. But there are few bowlers as professional as Mike Hendrick and the pitches on which we played Test cricket on would have suited him down to the ground – a wet one at Sydney, one with pace and bounce at Perth, the one at Melbourne where a bowler had to be tight and accurate. He would have done well in India too.

Hendo also has a very important psychological effect on the team. He always gives a hundred and one per cent and, just as vital, he always looks as though he's putting everything into his game. When you watch him you know he is really trying and that helps to lift your own performance. Hendo's very much an unsung hero as far as England are concerned.

Young Graham Dilley found himself thrown in at the deep end and bowled well without taking a lot of wickets. He bowls wide of the crease and is very chest-on at delivery – and I think he must improve his action if he is to become a top-class Test player.

Bob Willis had lost a yard and I'm afraid that at that pace he looked a very ordinary Test Match bowler. He doesn't move the ball away from the batsman much, so unless he has a real edge of speed he will struggle to take wickets at Test level. The one-day game, where economy and accuracy are much more important, is another matter altogether, and he excelled.

England also suffered from a lack of all-rounders. Ian Botham's bowling performances were incredible at times – remember that marathon at Perth – but he hardly got into the Australian tour as a batsman until the last Test in Melbourne where he scored a fine century, when even that was too late to do England much good. In the one-day matches he seemed to go berserk at times, trying to hoist straight deliveries over square-leg. He simply refused to believe that the bowling was as straight as it was and kept wondering why he was getting out lbw; we told him often enough but it didn't do much good. In the Test Matches he usually made the mistake of trying to hit the cover off the ball before he had settled in. Even when we were in trouble and obviously wanted somebody to stay in, he would bash a catch to cover point as though it was the last over of a Sunday match. It was a hell of a waste.

Geoff Miller made little impact on the tour before he had to return home injured – we could certainly have done with him playing well – and Bob Taylor didn't get enough runs to rate as an all-rounder. Peter Willey played very well in the one-day series but did nothing in the Test Matches; he kept getting out early on so you have to wonder how much his game is dominated by limited-overs philosophy. As it worked out the four men who should have been regarded as all-rounders – Botham, Miller, Willey and Taylor – made virtually no impact on the Tests with their batting, and that was a major disadvantage.

Before the tour started Derek Underwood was being described by some as the best left-arm spinner in the world, and when I suggested Phil Edmonds would do just as good a job for us since he was a better fielder and batsman there was quite a fuss about it. I think the tour proved me right. Great bowler that he is, Derek didn't bowl nearly as well as we had hoped. Perhaps his two years with WSC hadn't done him much good (because fast bowlers tended to dominate in their matches) or perhaps the tour itinerary was against him because he's the sort of bowler who likes to bowl and bowl; whatever the reasons he wasn't the old Derek Underwood. He seemed unable to come back and bowl a second spell well, as though he lacked the stamina, and he bowled more bad deliveries on this one tour than I have seen him bowl in the rest of his career. When did anyone see Derek swept as often because he was wandering down the leg-side – and his whole bowling philosophy is based on the accuracy that frustrates and niggles batsmen into mistakes.

I think Derek was very disappointed with himself and won't look back on the tour with much satisfaction except for his wonderful rearguard batting performance at Sydney. He doesn't bat or field as well as Edmonds and it was significant that he was left out of the one-day finals, partly because it was felt the West Indies had the measure of him and partly because England were anxious about their own batting strengths.

Essex's John Lever has been on several tours and played relatively little; it's fashionable to look back and say he would have improved the team in that match or the other but the fact is that there seemed little pressure to put him in the side at the time. He's a fast-medium bowler with lots of stamina but with Willis slowing down and Botham the stock all-rounder we needed a bowler with genuine pace – and that is why Dilley was preferred each time. The composition of the party plus our injury problems made that inevitable and the only place where he should have played was in Sydney where it was obviously a seamer's pitch.

Our batting let us down far too often and I think you have to look at Ian Botham's batting in the light of the extra responsibilities given to him at the start of the tour. The management said they wanted to look to the future and Ian was made a member of the selection party, presumably to encourage him to think about the game and see what his ideas were. I'm not sure that it worked.

In Tests where the situation called for a sense of responsibility he showed very little and gradually he reached a stage where he was virtually at his wits' end. After getting out in a Sydney match he asked me to watch him in the nets and tell him what was wrong. I remember telling him: 'There's no mystery and I don't have to watch you in the nets. You are a bit too cocky and confident and you are playing too many shots before you get in. We all have to work for a few runs before we start to play shots and even you have to settle in before you start whacking it around.

Technically,' I continued, 'the one thing wrong is that you're standing too straight when you hit the ball. You're not bending your left knee, not getting your head over the ball and so you're bound to hit it in the air.'

He worked hard at it after that and it paid off with centuries in Melbourne and later in Bombay.

I felt that his attitude in the nets was poor. Considering he is an all-rounder you would have expected him to bowl, but he hardly ever bowled, he was perfectly happy to bat for ages expecting others to bowl at him – a fact which was pointed out to him rather bluntly by one or two of the other players towards the end of the tour.

Everyone expected David Gower to do well, not least because he had succeeded in Australia the previous year. I suspect he thought it would all be rather too easy, another inevitable piece in a rich pattern. Cricket doesn't automatically work that way.

My feeling was that he showed no discipline or application in any of his batting, playing like a man who had scored 30 before he had faced half a dozen deliveries. There were very few matches outside the Internationals in which to find form so his problem gradually got worse rather than better, and David doesn't help himself by that characteristically flip attitude. It looks as though he doesn't care and that certainly can't help his cause. 'I care all right and I think about it, but there's no point in moping around,' he told me once. Fair enough, up to a point – but his thinking was obviously miles wide of the mark because, apart from his 98 not out in the Second Test his performances fell way below his capabilities. He was out far too often driving without using his feet or pulling deliveries which were just short of a length and which he should have played defensively early in his innings. He seemed incapable of putting together a steady, sensible innings – it was shots all the way, disappointment all the way, and he never seemed to learn.

Whatever happened to Derek Randall? I'm sure he would like the answer to that one because the poor lad struggled so badly he was eventually unrecognizable as the hero of the Centenary Test. I think his problem was confidence – too much of it at first and not enough of it when the runs began to dry up.

Derek had played in Perth and was in good form when the tour started – 97 in the first match against Queensland underlined that. But his problems started in the First Test in Perth and I don't think it was coincidence.

He had played in Perth before and was full of stories about how fast the pitches were; he had developed this theory that the best way to play on quick, bouncy surfaces was to get away from the ball rather than in line. Now that is just the opposite from his normal style in which he usually shuffles across and covers his off stump – but he had developed this fixation and it kept getting him out. Once he had made three low scores he lost his confidence – and that was the finish for him because confidence is his chief asset.

Derek is not a technique player so he can't fall back on that when things start to go wrong. He must be positive and confident and play his shots, but the self-doubts grew in his mind as his poor run got longer and his form went from bad to worse. By the time the one-day finals came round he was virtually pleading with me to play – there was some doubt because I had a hand injury – and spare him the possibility of failing again. His confidence had gone completely.

The most interesting batsman on the tour for me was Graham Gooch who was working as hard at the end of the tour as he had in the first week. He trained hard, put in a lot of work at the nets and played very straight – and I was amazed when he was left out of the First Test Match. Graham is a very quiet, sleepy sort of individual who doesn't say too much but has a really funny sense of humour once you get him going. I reckon he had a very good tour and I was pleased when he left his mark with 99 and 51 on the Third Test; he deserved to do well.

Considering he played in only the one-day International matches David Bairstow can look back on the tour with tremendous satisfaction. He played several sterling innings, doing exactly the right job just when it was needed; his wicket-keeping was top-drawer and he convinced a lot of others what we in Yorkshire have known for years: that he is a real character with guts and personality who is not easily ignored or forgotten. David made a big impact on people wherever he went and can only have enhanced his England prospects.

But I'm not sure what happened to a player like Wayne Larkins. Through absolutely no fault of his own he barely got into the tour until the last few weeks; he had been picked to tour with England on merit, and half the country scarcely knew he was there. It was a great shame, the fault of a crazy itinerary and certainly no fault of his.

Mike Brearley's performance as a player – and I make a distinction between that and his ability as a captain – was in my opinion flattered and exaggerated by his figures at the end of the tour. Let's face it: Mike is one of the five specialist batsmen in the side and yet he goes in at seven. A travesty and an admission of his shortcomings which is lost on nobody.

England's batting overall was poor and by the time Mike got in with five wickets down we were usually in trouble. We needed somebody to graft and pull us round and I reckon he was lucky to be able to play the only way he knows – to push a couple here and there, grit it out, battle along with guts and determination which glossed over his lack of Test ability. The plain fact is that no side can afford to go into Test cricket these days knowing they are carrying anybody in terms of performance. Every player fails from time to time, hits a lean spell and so on, but it is absolute folly to persist in playing a man who is not up to the job as a Test player.

Mike's record as a captain is impressive enough and he said during that winter that he was ready to go on. When England sit down to consider the captaincy in future I hope they will change their thinking and do what the Australians do – select the twelve best men, nominate a captain from them and tell him to get on with the job. That's not a new notion as far as I am concerned; I have always thought there's more than a touch of who you are rather than how well you can perform. England seem to have a fixation with so-called leadership qualities – and it has usually meant background. Australia think in terms of performance first and foremost, and they have been the most successful Test Match country throughout the years, so they must know a thing or two.

In the last Test at Melbourne we put on 116 before the first wicket fell and when we came out after lunch Greg Chappell realized things were going against Aussie and he had to do something about it. His language as we walked on to the pitch was colourful to say the least; players were snapped at by their surnames or told in no uncertain terms what to do and how to do it; there was no friendliness or false bonhomie. He was wielding a big stick and he expected his players to respond like men. If an England captain acted like that there would be hell to pay – and I doubt if he would keep his job for long however successful his record. But Australia won the series 3–0. Their philosophy can't be all that bad.

In my view Mike's casual sort of captaincy encouraged what I regarded as a bad lack of discipline and a hit-or-miss attitude during the tour and that time-keeping was bad; we always seemed to be hanging around waiting for somebody, and the nets were often organized in a lackadaisical fashion.

Ken Barrington as assistant manager was supposed to be in charge of net practices and he's a real expert at it – there was plenty of evidence of that on our tour to Australia in 1978/79. I'm not knocking Kenny, but he certainly didn't seem to exert the same influence as before (did somebody tell him not to?). He seemed to run the nets as a time-keeper rather than as a coach. His experience simply wasn't used enough and neither in my opinion was Alec Bedser's knowledge. They are a bit old-fashioned and some of the players tend to laugh at them in a good-natured way from time to time. But virtues like discipline, punctuality and a willingness to help each other are pretty old-fashioned virtues and I reckon England could have done with more of them. Perhaps things seemed worse than they were because we were losing – but surely that's when you have to pull together twice as hard and really knuckle down to the job as professionals.

It reached a stage during the Melbourne Test where I went to nets at 9.50 pm – not much more than an hour before the start of play – and there wasn't a single player ready to bowl. Three of the lads not playing in the match had only just arrived at the ground and weren't even changed.

Bad time-keeping, lack of attention to detail, sloppy attitudes, lack of professionalism ... I don't take any pleasure in recording the fact that there was far too much of all of them. We needed to be at the top of our form and in the right mental shape because Australia were obviously a good side. Taking the tour as a whole they certainly proved themselves the better team compared with England.

Australia had a world-class bowler in Lillee, who may have lost the edge of his pace but who is bowling more intelligently than ever. Rod Marsh has seen a lot of Lillee over the years and he reckons he is better now than he has ever been. His performance in the Melbourne Test was the best of his career – and nobody would disagree with that. The Chappell brothers are both world-class batsmen. Kim Hughes is improving all the time, and Border played very well indeed. Their batting in the Tests always looked more solid and reliable than ours. Geoff Dymock bowled very well as we knew he would and Len Pascoe is probably the most underrated of their bowlers at present; he's quick, strong and determined.

What struck me as a bit ironic, in view of the pre-publicity which suggested the youngsters were going to dominate, was the way in which the old lags of the party turned in the most consistent performances – Lillee, Dymock, the Chappell brothers – and I didn't do too badly either.

Looking back, it is clear to everybody that Australia cannot take another tour like the one we and West Indies put together. They have had a surfeit of cricket, the stars have lost a lot of their glitter through playing in front of Aussie audiences repeatedly in the past three years, and the public seems satiated. Crowds of 20,000 in Melbourne might sound a lot in relative terms but they are in fact very poor for Melbourne.

The 1979–80 winter tour simply involved too much travelling and not enough cricket. They must revise the itinerary to involve more first-class matches because that is the only way a touring party can keep all its players in some kind of form and practice. Our reserve players got very little cricket in the middle and it was quite soul-destroying for them.

Records of the One-day series and the Test series

Benson and Hedges World Series Cup One-Day Internationals

AUSTRALIA v. WEST INDIES
Played at Sydney, 27 November 1979. Australia won by 5 wkts.

ENGLAND v. WEST INDIES
Played at Sydney, 28 November 1979. England won by 2 runs.

ENGLAND

D. W. Randall	c Parry b Garner	49
†J. M. Brearley	c Greenidge b Parry	25
D. I. Gower	b Croft	44
G. A. Gooch	c & b Parry	2
P. Willey	not out	58
I. T. Botham	b Garner	11
‡D. L. Bairstow	c Murray b Garner	0
G. Miller	b Roberts	4
G. R. Dilley	run out	1
D. L. Underwood R. G. D. Willis	} did not bat	
Extras	(B4 LB13)	17
Total (50 overs)	(8 wkts.)	211

BOWLING

	O	M	R	W
Roberts	9	0	37	1
Holding	9	0	47	0
Croft	10	0	34	1
Garner	10	0	31	3
Parry	10	0	35	2
Kallicharran	2	0	10	0

FALL OF WICKETS
79–1, 88–2, 91–3, 160–4, 195–5, 195–6, 210–7, 211–8

WEST INDIES

C. G. Greenidge	c Willis b Miller	42
D. L. Haynes	b Dilley	4
L. G. Rowe	lbw b Willis	60
A. I. Kallicharran	not out	44
†C. H. Lloyd	c Brearley b Willis	4
‡D. L. Murray	c Gower b Underwood	3
D. R. Parry	b Underwood	4
A. M. E. Roberts	c Randall b Underwood	16
J. Garner	not out	8
M. A. Holding	c Gower b Underwood	0
C. E. H. Croft	b Botham	3
Extras	(B1 LB7)	8
Total (47 overs)		196

BOWLING

	O	M	R	W
Dilley	6	2	21	1
Botham	7	1	26	1
Underwood	10	0	44	4
Miller	10	0	33	1
Willey	8	0	29	0
Willis	6	0	35	2

FALL OF WICKETS
19–1, 68–2, 132–3, 143–4, 144–5, 155–6, 177–7, 185–8, 186–9

Rain affected this match, so the West Indies were set 199 runs for victory in 47 overs. West Indies won the toss. Peter Willey was Man of the Match.
Crowd: 6,120

ENGLAND v. AUSTRALIA
Played at Melbourne, 8 December 1979. England won by 3 wkts.

AUSTRALIA

J. M. Wiener	b Botham	7
B. M. Laird	lbw b Dilley	7
A. R. Border	c Willey b Dilley	29
†G. S. Chappell	c Gooch b Willey	92
K. J. Hughes	st Bairstow b Gooch	23
K. D. Walters	c Randall b Gooch	12
‡R. W. Marsh	c Bairstow b Willey	14
R. J. Bright	c Gooch b Willey	1
D. K. Lillee	not out	13
R. M. Hogg	c Brearley b Underwood	1
J. R. Thomson	did not bat	
Extras	(B1 LB5 NB2)	8
Total (50 overs)	(9 wkts.)	207

BOWLING

	O	M	R	W
Dilley	10	1	30	2
Botham	9	2	27	1
Willis	7	0	28	0
Gooch	6	0	32	2
Underwood	10	0	49	1
Willey	8	0	33	3

FALL OF WICKETS
15–1, 15–2, 73–3, 114–4, 145–5, 184–6, 193–7, 193–8, 207–9

ENGLAND

D. W. Randall	lbw b Bright	28
G. Boycott	c Lillee b Hogg	68
P. Willey	c Marsh b Hogg	37
D. I. Gower	c Marsh b Lillee	17
G. A. Gooch	run out	1
I. T. Botham	c Walters b Hogg	10
†J. M. Brearley	c Marsh b Lillee	27
‡D. L. Bairstow	not out	15
G. R. Dilley	not out	0
D. L. Underwood	} did not bat	
R. G. D. Willis		
Extras	(LB3 NB3)	6
Total (49 overs)	(7 wkts.)	209

BOWLING

	O	M	R	W
Lillee	10	1	36	2
Hogg	10	2	26	3
Thomson	10	1	49	0
Chappell	8	0	40	0
Bright	9	1	40	1
Walters	2	0	12	0

FALL OF WICKETS
71–1, 134–2, 137–3, 138–4, 148–5, 183–6, 203–7

England won the toss. G. S. Chappell was Man of the Match.
Crowd: 24,726

AUSTRALIA v. WEST INDIES
Played at Melbourne, 9 December 1979. West Indies won by 80 runs.

ENGLAND v. AUSTRALIA
Played at Sydney, 11 December 1979. England won by 72 runs.

ENGLAND

D. W. Randall	run out	42
G. Boycott	b Lillee	105
P. Willey	c Walker b Chappell	64
D. I. Gower	c Wiener b Lillee	7
G. A. Gooch	b Thomson	11
I. T. Botham	c Walters b Lillee	5
‡D. L. Bairstow	c sub (Hookes) b Lillee	18
†J. M. Brearley	not out	2
D. L. Underwood	} did not bat	
G. R. Dilley		
R. G. D. Willis		
Extras	(LB6 W1 NB3)	10
Total (49 overs)	(7 wkts)	264

BOWLING

	O	M	R	W
Lillee	10	0	56	4
Thomson	9	0	53	1
Walker	10	1	30	0
Laughlin	8	0	39	0
Border	4	0	24	0
Chappell	5	0	28	1
Walters	3	0	24	0

FALL OF WICKETS
78–1, 196–2, 220–3, 236–4, 242–5, 245–6, 264–7

AUSTRALIA

J. M. Wiener	st Bairstow b Willey	14
W. M. Darling	c Randall b Willis	20
A. R. Border	b Willey	1
†G. S. Chappell	run out	0
K. J. Hughes	c Bairstow b Willis	1
K. D. Walters	c Bairstow b Botham	34
‡R. W. Marsh	b Dilley	12
T. J. Laughlin	c Gooch b Randall	74
D. K. Lillee	b Botham	14
J. R. Thomson	run out	0
M. H. N. Walker	not out	9
Extras	(LB10 W2 NB1)	13
Total (47.2 overs)		192

BOWLING

	O	M	R	W
Dilley	9	0	29	1
Botham	10	1	36	2
Willis	10	1	32	2
Willey	5	0	18	2
Underwood	6	1	29	0
Gooch	7	0	33	0
Randall	0.2	0	2	1

FALL OF WICKETS
33–1, 36–2, 36–3, 38–4, 39–5, 63–6, 115–7, 146–8, 147–9

England won the toss. Geoffrey Boycott was Man of the Match.
Crowd: 15,083

AUSTRALIA v. WEST INDIES
Played at Sydney, 21 December 1979. Australia won by 7 runs.

ENGLAND v. WEST INDIES
Played at Brisbane, 23 December 1979. West Indies won by 9 wkts.

ENGLAND

D. W. Randall	c Lloyd b Roberts	0
G. Boycott	c sub (Marshall) b Holding	68
P. Willey	run out	34
D. I. Gower	c Holding b Roberts	59
G. A. Gooch	b Garner	17
I. T. Botham	lbw b Holding	4
‡D. L. Bairstow	c Lloyd b Roberts	12
†J. M. Brearley	not out	9
G. R. Dilley	b Garner	0
D. L. Underwood	} did not bat	
R. G. D. Willis		
Extras	(LB8 W5 NB1)	14
Total (50 overs)	(8 wkts.)	217

BOWLING

	O	M	R	W
Roberts	10	3	26	3
Holding	10	1	44	2
Garner	10	0	37	2
Richards	10	0	44	0
King	10	0	52	0

FALL OF WICKETS
0–1, 70–2, 167–3, 174–4, 191–5, 205–6, 209–7, 217–8

WEST INDIES

C. G. Greenidge	not out	85
D. L. Haynes	c Underwood b Gooch	41
I. V. A. Richards	not out	85
L. G. Rowe		
A. I. Kallicharran		
†C. H. Lloyd		
C. L. King		
‡D. L. Murray	} did not bat	
A. M. E. Roberts		
M. A. Holding		
J. Garner		
Extras	(LB4 NB3)	7
Total (46.5 overs)	(1 wkt.)	218

BOWLING

	O	M	R	W
Botham	10	1	39	0
Dilley	8	1	25	0
Willis	10	2	27	0
Underwood	9	0	43	0
Willey	6	0	39	0
Gooch	3.5	0	38	1

FALL OF WICKETS
109–1

West Indies won the toss. C. G. Greenidge was Man of the Match.
Crowd: 11,294

ENGLAND v. AUSTRALIA
Played at Sydney, 26 December 1979. England won by 4 wkts.

AUSTRALIA

B. M. Laird	b Botham	6
J. M. Wiener	c Bairstow b Botham...............	2
A. R. Border	c Gower b Gooch	22
†G. S. Chappell	run out	52
K. J. Hughes	b Willis	23
I. M. Chappell	not out	60
‡R. W. Marsh	c Bairstow b Dilley.................	10
D. K. Lillee	not out	2
R. M. Hogg		
G. Dymock.................	} did not bat	
L. S. Pascoe		
Extras...................	(B3 LB10 NB4)	17
Total (47 overs)........	(6 wkts.)............................	194

BOWLING

	O	M	R	W
Dilley	10	1	32	1
Botham	9	1	33	2
Willis	10	1	38	1
Underwood........	10	2	36	0
Gooch..............	8	0	38	1

FALL OF WICKETS
5–1, 21–2, 50–3, 109–4, 133–5, 179–6

ENGLAND

G. A. Gooch	lbw b Hogg	29
G. Boycott.................	not out	86
P. Willey..................	b Pascoe	51
D. I. Gower	c Marsh b Hogg	2
D. W. Randall..............	c G. Chappell b Pascoe	1
I. T. Botham	lbw b Hogg	6
†J. M. Brearley.............	c Marsh b Hogg	0
‡D. I. Bairstow.............	not out	7
G. R. Dilley		
D. L. Underwood	} did not bat	
R. G. D. Willis.............		
Extras...................	(LB1 W1 NB11)	13
Total (45.1 overs)......	(6 wkts.)............................	195

BOWLING

	O	M	R	W
Lillee................	10	0	47	0
Pascoe..............	10	2	28	2
Hogg................	10	0	46	4
Dymock	10	1	38	0
G. Chappell	5.1	0	23	0

FALL OF WICKETS
41–1, 152–2, 157–3, 170–4, 179–5, 179–6

Australia won the toss. Geoffrey Boycott was Man of the Match.
Crowd: 21,000

ENGLAND v. AUSTRALIA
Played at Sydney, 14 January 1980. England won by 2 wkts.

AUSTRALIA

J. M. Wiener	st Bairstow b Emburey	33
R. B. McCosker	c Brearley b Willey	41
I. M. Chappell	c Randall b Emburey	8
†G. S. Chappell	c Randall b Stevenson	34
K. J. Hughes	c Larkins b Lever	34
A. R. Border	c Bairstow b Lever	0
‡R. W. Marsh	c Bairstow b Stevenson	0
D. K. Lillee	lbw b Stevenson	0
G. Dymock	run out	0
J. R. Thomson	not out	3
L. S. Pascoe	b Stevenson	5
Extras	(LB1 W3 NB1)	5
Total (48.4 overs)		163

BOWLING

	O	M	R	W
Lever	9	1	11	2
Botham	7	0	33	0
Gooch	3	0	13	0
Stevenson	9.4	0	33	4
Emburey	10	1	33	2
Willey	10	0	35	1

FALL OF WICKETS
74–1, 82–2, 89–3, 148–4, 149–5, 150–6, 150–7, 152–8, 155–9

ENGLAND

G. A. Gooch	c McCosker b Pascoe	69
W. Larkins	c Thomson b Lillee	5
P. Willey	lbw b Lillee	0
D. I. Gower	c Marsh b Lillee	3
†J. M. Brearley	b G. Chappell	5
D. W. Randall	c Pascoe b G. Chappell	0
I. T. Botham	b Lillee	0
‡D. L. Bairstow	not out	21
J. E. Emburey	c G. Chappell b Dymock	18
G. B. Stevenson	not out	28
J. K. Lever	did not bat	
Extras	(LB5 W1 NB9)	15
Total (48.5 overs)	(8 wkts.)	164

BOWLING

	O	M	R	W
Thomson	9.5	0	46	0
Dymock	9	1	30	1
Lillee	10	6	12	4
Pascoe	10	0	38	1
G. Chappell	10	3	23	2

FALL OF WICKETS
31–1, 31–2, 40–3, 51–4, 56–5, 61–6, 105–7, 129–8

England won the toss. Dennis Lillee was Man of the Match.
Crowd: 12,000

RECORDS

ENGLAND v. WEST INDIES
Played at Adelaide, 16 January 1980. West Indies won by 107 runs.

WEST INDIES

C. G. Greenidge	c Emburey b Willey	50
D. L. Haynes	c Gooch b Stevenson	26
I. V. A. Richards	b Botham	88
A. I. Kallicharran	c & b Botham	57
C. L. King	run out	12
J. Garner	not out	7
A. M. E. Roberts	not out	0
†C. H. Lloyd		
‡D. L. Murray	} did not bat	
M. A. Holding		
L. G. Rowe		
Extras	(B1 LB4 NB1)	6
Total (50 overs)	(5 wkts.)	246

BOWLING

	O	M	R	W
Lever	10	1	54	0
Botham	10	0	35	2
Gooch	2	0	22	0
Stevenson	8	1	53	1
Emburey	10	0	39	0
Willey	10	1	37	1

FALL OF WICKETS
58–1, 115–2, 224–3, 227–4, 245–5

ENGLAND

G. A. Gooch	b King	20
†J. M. Brearley	c Murray b Roberts	0
P. Willey	c Lloyd b King	5
W. Larkins	c Lloyd b King	24
D. I. Gower	c sub (Croft) b King	12
D. W. Randall	b Roberts	16
I. T. Botham	c Haynes b Roberts	22
‡D. L. Bairstow	not out	23
G. B. Stevenson	b Roberts	1
J. E. Emburey	c Murray b Roberts	1
J. K. Lever	b Garner	11
Extras	(LB2 W1 NB1)	4
Total (42.5 overs)		139

BOWLING

	O	M	R	W
Roberts	10	5	22	5
Holding	7	0	16	0
King	9	3	23	4
Garner	7.5	3	9	1
Richards	7	0	46	0
Kallicharran	2	0	19	0

FALL OF WICKETS
5–1, 24–2, 31–3, 52–4, 68–5, 98–6, 100–7, 105–8, 109–9

England won the toss. A. M. E. Roberts was Man of the Match.
Crowd: 24,986

AUSTRALIA v. WEST INDIES
Played at Sydney, 18 January 1980. Australia won by 9 runs.

ENGLAND v. WEST INDIES
Played at Melbourne, 20 January 1980. West Indies won by 2 runs.

WEST INDIES

C. G. Greenidge	c Larkins b Botham	80
D. L. Haynes	c Bairstow b Willis	9
I. V. A. Richards	c Bairstow b Dilley	23
A. I. Kallicharran	b Botham	42
†C. H. Lloyd	b Botham	4
C. L. King	not out	31
‡D. L. Murray	c Bairstow b Dilley	4
A. M. E. Roberts	run out	1
J. Garner	run out	3
M. A. Holding	not out	5
C. E. H. Croft	did not bat	
Extras	(LB11 W1 NB1)	13
Total (50 overs)	(8 wkts.)	215

BOWLING

	O	M	R	W
Willis	10	1	51	1
Botham	10	2	33	3
Emburey	10	0	31	0
Dilley	10	0	39	2
Willey	10	0	48	0

FALL OF WICKETS

17–1, 66–2, 161–3, 168–4, 168–5, 181–6, 183–7, 197–8

ENGLAND

G. A. Gooch	c King b Holding	9
G. Boycott	c Greenidge b Roberts	35
P. Willey	run out	51
D. I. Gower	c Holding b Roberts	10
W. Larkins	run out	34
I. T. Botham	c Lloyd b Roberts	19
†J. M. Brearley	not out	25
‡D. I. Bairstow	run out	4
J. E. Emburey		
G. R. Dilley	} did not bat	
R. G. D. Willis		
Extras	(B12 LB12 W1 NB1)	26
Total (50 overs)	(7 wkts.)	213

BOWLING

	O	M	R	W
Roberts	10	1	30	3
Holding	10	1	43	1
Garner	10	1	27	0
Croft	10	1	23	0
King	4	0	30	0
Richards	6	1	34	0

FALL OF WICKETS

13–1, 74–2, 96–3, 152–4, 164–5, 190–6, 213–7

England won the toss.
Crowd: 29,000

ENGLAND v. WEST INDIES
Played at Sydney, 22 January 1980. West Indies won by 8 wickets.

ENGLAND

G. A. Gooch	lbw b Garner	23
G. Boycott	c Greenidge b Roberts	63
P. Willey	b Garner	3
D. I. Gower	c Murray b Holding	27
W. Larkins	b Croft	14
I. T. Botham	c King b Roberts	37
‡D. I. Bairstow	not out	18
†J. M. Brearley	run out	4
J. E. Emburey	run out	6
G. R. Dilley	} did not bat	
R. G. D. Willis		
Extras	(B1 LB11 NB1)	13
Total (50 overs)	(8 wkts.)	208

BOWLING

	O	M	R	W
Roberts	10	3	31	2
Holding	10	1	34	1
Croft	10	3	29	1
Garner	10	0	44	2
Richards	3	0	19	0
King	7	1	38	0

FALL OF WICKETS
40–1, 54–2, 118–3, 126–4, 155–5, 188–6, 194–7, 208–8

WEST INDIES

C. G. Greenidge	not out	98
D. L. Haynes	lbw b Botham	17
I. V. A. Richards	c Botham b Willey	65
A. I. Kallicharran	not out	8
†C. H. Lloyd		
C. L. King		
‡D. L. Murray		
M. A. Holding	} did not bat	
A. M. E. Roberts		
J. Garner		
C. E. H. Croft		
Extras	(B5 LB10 W5 NB1)	21
Total (47.3 overs)	(2 wkts.)	209

BOWLING

	O	M	R	W
Willis	10	0	35	0
Dilley	7	0	37	0
Botham	10	1	28	1
Emburey	9.3	0	48	0
Willey	10	2	35	1
Gooch	1	0	5	0

FALL OF WICKETS
16–1, 180–2

England won the toss. C. G. Greenidge was Man of the Finals.
I. V. A. Richards was Man of the Series.
Crowd: 20,000

The Test Matches:
FIRST TEST MATCH AUSTRALIA v. ENGLAND
Played at Perth, 14, 15, 16, 18 and 19 December 1979. Australia XI won by 138 runs.

AUSTRALIA

Batsman	First Innings		Second Innings	
J. M. Wiener	run out	11	c Randall b Underwood	58
B. M. Laird	lbw b Botham	0	c Taylor b Underwood	33
A. R. Border	lbw b Botham	4	c Taylor b Willis	115
†G. S. Chappell	c Boycott b Botham	19	st Taylor b Underwood	43
K. J. Hughes	c Brearley b Underwood	99	c Miller b Botham	4
P. M. Toohey	c Underwood b Dilley	19	c Taylor b Botham	3
‡R. W. Marsh	c Taylor b Dilley	42	c Gower b Botham	4
R. J. Bright	c Taylor b Botham	17	lbw b Botham	12
D. K. Lillee	c Taylor b Botham	18	c Willey b Dilley	19
G. Dymock	b Botham	5	not out	20
J. R. Thomson	not out	1	b Botham	8
Extras	(B4 LB3 NB2)	9	(B4 LB5 W2 NB7)	18
Total		244		337

BOWLING

	O	M	R	W	O	M	R	W
Dilley	18	1	47	2	18	3	50	1
Botham	35	9	78	6	45.5	14	98	5
Willis	23	7	47	0	26	7	52	1
Underwood	13	4	33	1	41	14	82	3
Miller	11	2	30	0	10	0	36	0
Willey					1	0	1	0

FALL OF WICKETS
2–1, 17–2, 20–3, 88–4, 127–5, 186–6, 219–7, 219–8, 243–9
91–1, 100–2, 168–3, 183–4, 191–5, 204–6, 225–7, 303–8, 323–9

ENGLAND

Batsman	First Innings		Second Innings	
D. W. Randall	c Hughes b Lillee	0	lbw b Dymock	1
G. Boycott	lbw b Lillee	0	not out	99
P. Willey	c Chappell b Dymock	9	lbw b Dymock	12
D. I. Gower	c Marsh b Lillee	17	c Thomson b Dymock	23
G. Miller	c Hughes b Thomson	25	c Chappell b Thomson	8
†J. M. Brearley	c Marsh b Lillee	64	(7) c Marsh b Bright	11
I. T. Botham	c Toohey b Thomson	15	(6) c Marsh b Lillee	18
‡R. W. Taylor	b Chappell	14	b Lillee	15
G. R. Dilley	not out	38	c Marsh b Dymock	16
D. L. Underwood	lbw b Dymock	13	c Wiener b Dymock	0
R. G. D. Willis	b Dymock	11	c Chappell b Dymock	0
Extras	(LB7 NB15)	22	(LB3 W1 NB8)	12
Total		228		215

BOWLING

	O	M	R	W	O	M	R	W
Lillee	28	11	73	4	23	5	74	2
Dymock	29.1	14	52	3	17.2	4	34	6
Chappell	11	6	5	1	6	4	6	0
Thomson	21	3	70	2	11	3	30	1
Bright	1	0	6	0	23	11	30	1
Wiener					8	3	22	0
Border					2	0	7	0

FALL OF WICKETS
0–1, 12–2, 14–3, 41–4, 74–5, 90–6, 123–7, 185–8, 203–9
8–1, 26–2, 64–3, 75–4, 115–5, 141–6, 182–7, 211–8, 211–9

England won the toss. Ian Botham was Man of the Match.

SECOND TEST MATCH
Played at Sydney, 4, 5, 6 and 8 January 1980. Australia XI won by 6 wkts.

ENGLAND

Batsman	First innings		Second innings	
G. A. Gooch	b Lillee	18	c G. Chappell by Dymock	4
G. Boycott	b Dymock	8	c McCosker b Pascoe	18
D. W. Randall	c G. Chappell b Lillee	0	(6) c Marsh b G. Chappell	25
P. Willey	c Wiener b Dymock	8	(3) b Pascoe	3
†J. M. Brearley	c Pascoe b Dymock	7	(4) c Marsh b Pascoe	19
D. I. Gower	b G. Chappell	3	(7) not out	98
I. T. Botham	c G. Chappell b Pascoe	27	(8) c Wiener b G. Chappell	0
‡R. W. Taylor	c Marsh b Lillee	10	(9) b Lillee	8
G. R. Dilley	not out	22	(1) b Dymock	4
R. G. D. Willis	c Wiener b Dymock	3	(11) c G. Chappell b Lillee	1
D. L. Underwood	c Border b Lillee	12	(5) c Border b Dymock	43
Extras	(NB 5)	5	(B1 LB10 W1 NB2)	14
Total		123		237

BOWLING

	O	M	R	W	O	M	R	W
Lillee	13.3	4	40	4	24.3	3	63	2
Dymock	17	6	42	4	28	8	48	3
Pascoe	9	4	14	1	23	3	76	3
G. Chappell	4	1	19	1	21	10	36	2
Higgs	1	0	3	0				

FALL OF WICKETS
10–1, 13–2, 31–3, 38–4, 41–5, 74–6, 75–7, 90–8, 98–9

6–1, 21–2, 29–3, 77–4, 105–5, 156–6, 174–7, 211–8, 218–9

AUSTRALIA

Batsman	First innings		Second innings	
R. B. McCosker	c Gower b Willis	1	(2) c Taylor b Underwood	41
J. M. Wiener	run out	22	(1) b Underwood	13
I. M. Chappell	c Brearley b Gooch	42	c Botham b Underwood	9
†G. S. Chappell	c Taylor b Underwood	3	not out	98
K. J. Hughes	c Taylor b Botham	18	c Dilley b Willis	47
A. R. Border	c Gooch b Botham	15	not out	2
‡R. W. Marsh	c Underwood b Gooch	7		
D. K. Lillee	c Brearley b Botham	5		
G. Dymock	c Taylor b Botham	4		
L. S. Pascoe	not out	10		
J. D. Higgs	b Underwood	2		
Extras	(B2 LB12 W2)	16	(LB8 W1)	9
Total		145	(4 wkts.)	219

BOWLING

	O	M	R	W	O	M	R	W
Botham	17	7	29	4	23.3	12	43	0
Willis	11	3	30	1	12	2	26	1
Underwood	13.2	3	39	2	26	6	71	3
Dilley	5	1	13	0	12	0	33	0
Willey	1	0	2	0	4	0	17	0
Gooch	11	4	16	2	8	2	20	0

FALL OF WICKETS
18–1, 52–2, 71–3, 92–4, 100–5, 114–6, 121–7, 129–8, 132–9

31–1, 51–2, 98–3, 203–4

Australia won the toss. G. S. Chappell was Man of the Match.

THIRD TEST MATCH

Played at Melbourne, 1, 2, 3, 5 and 6 February 1980. Australia XI won by 8 wkts.

ENGLAND

G. A. Gooch	run out	99	b Mallett	51
G. Boycott	c Mallett b Dymock	44	b Lillee	7
W. Larkins	c G. Chappell b Pascoe	25	lbw b Pascoe	3
D. I. Gower	lbw b Lillee	0	b Lillee	11
P. Willey	lbw b Pascoe	1	c Marsh b Lillee	2
I. T. Botham	c Marsh b Lillee	8	(7) not out	119
†J. M. Brearley	not out	60	(6) c Border b Pascoe	10
‡R. W. Taylor	b Lillee	23	c Border b Lillee	32
D. L. Underwood	c I. Chappell b Lillee	3	b Pascoe	0
J. K. Lever	b Lillee	22	c Marsh b Lillee	12
R. G. D. Willis	c G. Chappell b Lillee	4	c G. Chappell b Pascoe	2
Extras	(B1 LB2 NB14)	17	(B2 LB12 NB10)	24
Total		306		273

BOWLING

	O	M	R	W	O	M	R	W
Lillee	33.1	9	60	6	33	6	78	5
Dymock	28	6	54	1	11	2	30	0
Mallett	35	9	104	0	14	1	45	1
Pascoe		7	71	2	29.5	3	80	4
Border					4	0	16	0

FALL OF WICKETS

116–1, 170–2, 175–3, 177–4, 177–5, 192–6, 238–7, 242–8, 296–9

25–1, 46–2, 64–3, 67–4, 88–5, 92–6, 178–7, 179–8, 268–9

AUSTRALIA

R. B. McCosker	c Botham b Underwood	33	lbw b Botham	2
B. M. Laird	c Gower b Underwood	74	c Boycott b Underwood	25
I. M. Chappell	c & b Underwood	75	not out	26
K. J. Hughes	c Underwood b Botham	15		
A. R. Border	c & b Lever	63		
†G. S. Chappell	c Larkins b Lever	114	(4) not out	40
‡R. W. Marsh	c Botham b Lever	17		
D. K. Lillee	c Willey b Lever	8		
G. Dymock	b Botham	19		
A. A. Mallett	lbw b Botham	25		
L. S. Pascoe	not out	1		
Extras	(B13 LB12 W1 NB7)	33	(LB8 NB2)	10
Total		477	(2 wkts.)	103

BOWLING

	O	M	R	W	O	M	R	W
Lever	53	15	111	4	7.4	3	18	0
Botham	39.5	15	105	3	12	5	18	1
Willis	21	4	61	0	5	3	8	0
Underwood	53	19	131	3	14	2	49	1
Willey	13	2	36	0				

FALL OF WICKETS

52–1, 179–2, 196–3, 219–4, 345–5, 411–6, 421–7, 432–8, 465–9

20–1, 42–2

England won the toss. Dennis Lillee was Man of the Match, and also Man of the Series.

Acknowledgements

The photographs in this book are reproduced by kind permission of the following:

Central Press Photos Ltd: pages 42(b), 43(b), 57(t/r).

Patrick Eagar: pages 20, 36, 50(t), 55, 57(t/l & b), 60, 63, 66, 69(t), 73(t/l & b/l), 74, 81(b), 84(t/r & b/l), 88(t/r & b), 91(t & b/r), 93(b), 96(t), 107, 111, 124, 152.

Jack Hickes: page 12(b).

McDonald's Systems of Australia: © page 108.

Adrian Murrell, All-Sport Photographic Ltd: pages 2, 10, 31(t), 43(t), 46, 47, 50(b), 53, 62, 73(b/r), 76, 81(t), 88(t/l), 93(t), 117, 119, 127, 129(b), 134(b), 143, 159, 160, 163.

News Ltd, Sydney: page 16.

Eric Piper, *Daily Mirror*: pages 12(t), 69(b), 73(t/r), 129(t), 132, 134(t), 136.

The Press Association Ltd: pages 31(b), 34, 39(t/l), 40, 42(t), 91(b/l), 96(b).

Sport & General Press Agency: page 39(t/r & b).

Sporting Pictures (UK) Ltd: page 84(b/r).

West of England Newspapers Ltd: page 84(t/l).